THE
Thomas A. Meyers
TECHNICAL ANALYSIS COURSE
Revised Edition

A Winning Program for Investors & Traders

PROBUS PUBLISHING COMPANY
Chicago, Illinois
Cambridge, England

Table of Contents

How to Take This Course

The objective of this course is to teach you technical analysis techniques that will enable you to preserve capital and boost investment profits, while at the same time minimizing risk of losses. It consists of text material for you to read and quizzes to complete. The quizzes are designed to reinforce the concepts brought out in the text portion and to enable you to evaluate your progress.

I recommend that you work at this course systematically. Only by reading the text and taking the quizzes at a regular and steady pace will you get the most out of this course and retain what you have learned.

The Text

The most important component of this course is the text. It is here that the concepts and techniques of technical analysis are first presented.

Reading each lesson twice will increase the likelihood of your understanding the text fully. In your first reading, concentrate on getting an overview of the lesson's contents. Pay attention to the headings and subheadings. Find the general theme of each section and see how that theme relates to others. Don't let yourself get bogged down with details during the first reading. Simply concentrate on remembering and understanding the major themes.

In your second reading, look for the details that underlie the themes. Read the entire lesson carefully and methodically, underlining key points, working out the details of the examples, and making marginal notations as you go.

The Quizzes

After reading a lesson and before going on to the next, work through the quiz at the end of the lesson. Answering the questions and comparing your own answers to those given will assist you in grasping the major ideas of that lesson. If you perform these self-check exercises conscientiously, you will develop a framework in which to place material presented in later lessons. This building process will help clarify the reading and, most important, will help you to apply what you have learned under real market conditions.

The Lessons

Similar to a carpenter, the technician has a variety of tools in his or her toolbox. Some basic tools (like bar charts and moving averages) are used quite frequently, while other more specialized and sophisticated tools (like relative strength index and stochastics) are used less often. Like a carpenter, each technician has his or her favorite tools, those which have been mastered through experience over time.

Each lesson in this course builds on the prior ones, providing you with the tools you need, from basic to complex, to become a master technician. Lesson 1 introduces you to technical analysis and explains the principles on which it is based. Lessons 2 through 15 teach you how to construct charts, spot profitable chart patterns, and use a variety of basic and advanced technical analysis tools. Techniques for determining the trend of the overall stock market are provided in Lessons 16 and 17. Finally, the last two lessons (18 and 19) pull all the pieces together by first, showing you how to use the various technical analysis tools in a structured approach to investment analysis and, second, providing an actual market case study.

For your benefit, important sources of technical analysis related information are described in the appendix. In addition, key terms used throughout this course are defined in the glossary.

INTRODUCTION

The Philosophy of Technical Analysis

Those "in the know" on Wall Street have increasingly turned to technical analysis in recent years. They realize that security prices do not move randomly, rather they move in repeating and identifiable patterns. They use this information to gain an edge on other investors and make money in the stock market. This course will enable others to do the same by making profitable investment decisions based on proven technical analysis techniques.

The Basic Principles

Before learning about the specific tools and techniques the technician (as one who employs technical analysis is called) uses to analyze various investment opportunities, it is essential that one understand the principles upon which technical analysis is based. The three key principles are:

1. Everything is discounted and reflected in market prices.
2. Prices move in trends and trends persist.
3. Market action is repetitive.

Let's examine each principle in detail.

The first and most important principle is that everything is discounted and reflected in market prices. The technician believes that all knowledge, regardless of type (fundamental, economic, political, psychological, or other), is already reflected in market prices. Technicians, unlike fundamental analysts, feel it is futile to study company financial statements, earnings and dividend reports, industry developments, and other data in an attempt to determine the "intrinsic value" of a stock or other market instrument. An example will illustrate why. During 1980, one share of CSX Corporation (see Table 1–1) was worth between $13.75 and $16.50, well below the book value per share of $23.44 (end of year). During 1987, the market price per share ranged from $22.175 to $41.75 or 29 percent below to 34 percent above the book value per share of $31.26. During 1992, the stock traded as high as $72.75 per share, more than twice the book value per share of $33.86. This wide divergence between the intrinsic value and actual market price is not the exception; it is commonplace. Technicians believe that the real value of a share of CSX Corporation at any point in time is determined solely by supply and demand, as reflected in trades made at the New York Stock Exchange.

Price movements are simply the reflection of changes in supply and demand. The technician does not care what the underlying forces of a shift in supply and demand are, rather he or she is interested in what occurs. If demand is greater than supply, prices will increase. On the other hand, if supply is greater than demand, prices will decline. *The study of market prices is all that is necessary.*

Table 1–1
Market Price versus Book Value for CSX Corporation
(Per Share Data ($)—Adjusted for 1983 Stock Split)

| | Book | Market Price | |
Year	Value	High	Low
1980	23.44	16.500	13.750
1981	25.31	20.250	13.750
1982	26.83	19.750	12.125
1983	31.00	27.500	16.000
1984	32.82	26.250	18.375
1985	30.15	31.875	22.375
1986	31.64	37.500	25.625
1987	31.38	41.750	22.125
1988	30.59	32.500	24.375
1989	33.24	38.625	29.750
1990	35.93	38.125	26.000
1991	31.08	58.000	29.750
1992	33.86	72.750	54.500

TECHNICAL ANALYSIS TIP — There is an old saying on Wall Street that goes "Sell on good news." Why should you sell on good news? Because if the actual news is as expected, it is, of course, already discounted and reflected in the market price. Therefore, you would expect no further rise in price based on that news.

The second principle on which technical analysis is based is that prices move in trends and trends persist. The supply and demand balance sets a trend in motion. Once in motion, a trend remains intact until it ends. For example, if a stock's price is moving up, it will continue its rise until there is a clear reversal. Likewise, if a stock is moving down, it will decline until a reversal.

An analogy will further clarify the second principle. When a car is parked in a garage, it is, in essence, trendless because it is not moving in a given direction. Assume a car is driven on to a street moving northbound. When the driver first turns on to that street, he or she is moving slowly but gradually picks up speed until a speed of 50 miles per hour is reached. The direction or trend is northbound. In order to change direction (or trend) to southbound, the driver would first have to slow down from 50 miles per hour, to perhaps five miles per hour, and turn around (or, perhaps, stop and drive in reverse). The driver could not instantly change direction (or trend), and if someone was following, this following motorist would be signalled by the slowing down before the first driver reversed direction (or trend).

Market prices move in a similar manner. First, they begin in one direction, up or down, creating a trend. That trend persists until the price movement slows and gives warning before finally reversing and moving in the opposite direction. At that point a new trend is initiated. As illustrated in Figure 1–1, trends can be readily spotted on charts. The chart patterns show the balance of supply and demand for a particular stock or other market instrument.

TECHNICAL ANALYSIS TIP — The old Wall Street adage "the trend is your friend" is true because, once begun, a trend is likely to continue. By following it you increase your probability of making money.

The final key principle on which technical analysis is based is that market action is repetitive. Certain patterns appear time after time on charts. These patterns have meanings that can be interpreted in terms of probable future price movement. Although not infallible, the odds are in their favor.

Figure 1–1
Example of Uptrend in Stock Prices

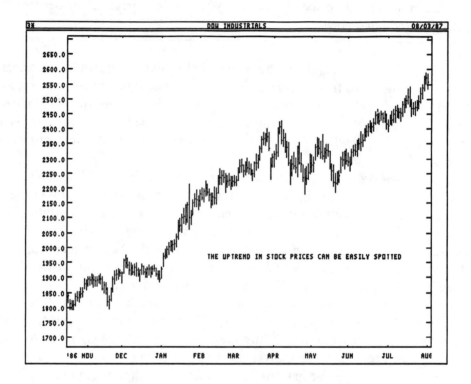

Human nature is such that it tends to react to similar situations in consistent ways. As a rule, people will act the same as they have in the past. Since the stock market is a reflection of the actions of people, technicians study it to determine how people will react under certain conditions and, thus, how security prices will move. Technicians analyze the recurrence of similar characteristics in an attempt to identify major market tops and bottoms.

Technical Analysis Defined

Giving consideration to the principles discussed, technical analysis can be defined as simply the study of individual securities and the overall market based on supply and demand. Technicians record, usually in chart form, historical price and volume activity and deduce from that pictured history the probable future trend of prices.

Adaptability to Different Markets and Investment Time Horizons

The beauty of technical analysis is that it can be applied effectively to virtually any trading medium and investment time horizon. A technician can analyze stocks, bonds, options, mutual funds, commodities, and many other forms of investments for buy and sell opportunities. And one can do so by examining tic-by-tic, intraday, daily, weekly, monthly, or some other interval of data to use technical analysis for a wide range of time horizons — from very short-term to very long-term perspectives.

The best manner in which to use technical analysis depends on one's approach to the market. Keep in mind that everyone invests differently. We all have different levels of stress, different temperaments, and different amounts of capital. It is important to apply technical analysis in a manner that complements one's own personality and individual investment philosophy. Obviously, those whose time, nerves, and capital are limited will want to pass up very short-term trading opportunities (such as intraday trading of stock index futures) and, perhaps, use longer-term technical analysis derived buy and sell signals for stocks or mutual funds. By recognizing one's individual investment strengths and weaknesses, users of technical analysis can find the trading medium and time horizons that are best for their individual investment situations.

True or False Quiz

Circle T if the statement is true or F if the statement is false.

T   F   1. Technicians study company financial statements and earnings and dividend reports to determine the value of a stock.

T   F   2. Technicians believe that supply and demand determine the real value of a share of stock at any point in time.

T   F   3. Technicians believe that the study of market prices is all that is necessary.

T   F   4. Prices move in trends and trends persist.

T   F   5. Trends in price typically change direction (either from up to down or down to up) without warning.

T   F   6. Trends can easily be identified on charts.

T   F   7. Market action is random in nature.

T   F   8. Technical analysis can be applied to stocks, but not commodities.

T   F   9. Technical analysis works better for short-term than long-term analysis.

Answers

1. *False.* Technicians believe it is futile to study fundamental data since it is already reflected in the market price of a stock.

2. *True.* Supply and demand, as reflected in actual trades typically made at a stock exchange, determine the market price (real value) of a company's stock at a given point in time.

3. *True.* Market prices reflect the supply and demand balance based on how investors act in certain situations.

4. *True.* This is the second principle upon which technical analysis is based.

5. *False.* Typically, prices moving either up or down will first decelerate the movement in the direction of the trend and then give warning prior to changing direction. Rarely does a trend reverse instantly.

6. *True.* See Figure 1–1 for an example.

7. *False.* Market action is repetitive and prices act in consistent ways under similar situations.

8. *False.* Technical analysis can be applied effectively to virtually any trading medium.

9. *False.* Although technical analysis is more often applied to short-term investment time horizons, it is equally effective in analyzing long-term trends.

CONSTRUCTING CHARTS

Basic Chart Construction

As shown in Lesson 1, technicians do not believe that the price of securities and the overall stock market move in a random manner. Rather, they contend that a direct relationship exists between price movements in the past and those that will occur in the future. Their objective is to determine what this relationship is so that they will be able to predict accurately whether the stock market or a particular security's price will go up or down.

The primary tool that a technician uses is a "picture" or chart of a stock's price movement.

Types of Charts

Technicians use four types of charts as illustrated in Figure 2–1. They are:

1. Bar chart.
2. Line (or close-only) chart.
3. Point and figure chart.
4. Japanese candlestick chart.

Bar charts are, by far, the most commonly used type of price chart. In a bar chart, a vertical line that ranges from the period's lowest price to its highest price represents each time period. A horizontal protrusion to the right marks the period's closing price.

Figure 2–1
Comparison of Bar Chart (Top-Left), Line Chart (Top-Right),
Point and Figure Chart (Bottom-Left),
and Japanese Candlestick Chart (Bottom-Right)

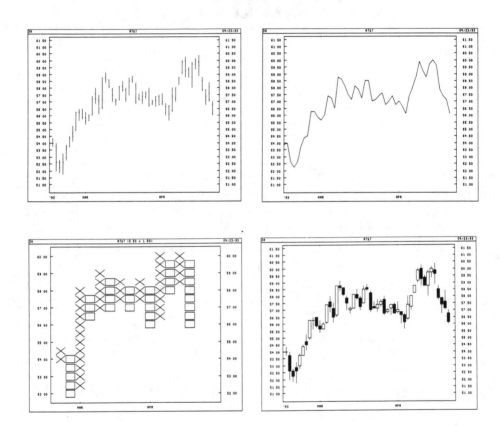

Some technicians believe that the closing price is the most important price of the trading day and, therefore, plot only closing prices in a line chart.

The third type of chart, the point and figure chart, will be examined in depth in Lesson 14. For now, note that it shows the same price information as the bar and line charts, but in a more compressed fashion. A rising price change is represented by an X, a declining movement by an O. Each X or O occupies a box on the chart and represents a price change of a certain magnitude.

The final type of chart, the Japanese candlestick chart, is so called because the lines resemble candles and wicks. For each period, the opening, high, low, and closing prices are plotted in a manner that will be explained fully in Lesson 15.

Regardless of the type of chart used, the length of the period examined will vary depending on whether one is oriented to short-term, intermediate-term, or long-term investments. Although there is no generally accepted definition of these three terms, short-term roughly refers to the next three months; intermediate-term is about three to six months from the present time; and long-term is considered to be approximately six months to one year from the current period. Technicians often use hourly and daily charts to determine the short-term trend of security price movements. They use weekly charts for gaining an intermediate-term perspective. And, monthly and yearly charts help technicians examine the long-term.

As noted earlier, bar charts are the most common type of chart used by technicians. Let's examine the bar chart in more detail.

The Bar Chart

Constructing a bar chart is easy as shown in Figure 2–2. A price scale is assigned to the vertical axis; a time scale (hourly, daily, weekly, etc.) is marked off on the horizontal axis. For each period, the high, low, and closing prices are plotted. Usually, opening price is also plotted for commodities but not for stocks. A vertical line, or bar, connects the high and low prices. Horizontal tics to the left and right of the bar represent the opening and closing prices, respectively.

Let's look at a more comprehensive example. Assume a stock traded at the prices shown in Table 2–1 over a period of five weeks (25 trading days). A daily bar chart of these prices is provided in Figure 2–3. A weekly bar chart (see Figure 2–4) of the same prices is simply a condensed version of the daily chart with each bar representing five days of price activity.

Figure 2–2
How a Bar Chart Is Constructed

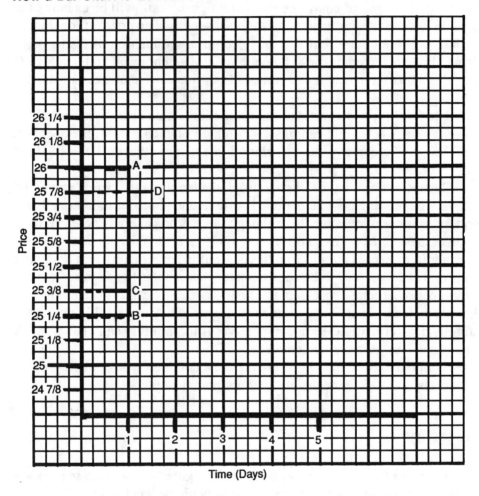

A: The high price for the day, $26
B: The low price for the day, $25¼
C: The opening price (not always on the bar chart), $25⅜
D: The closing price, $25⅞

Table 2–1
Data for Bar Chart Example

Date	High	Low	Close
February 22	115.625	113.125	115.250
February 23	115.875	114.375	115.375
February 24	116.750	114.750	116.125
February 25	117.875	114.125	114.500
February 26	115.750	114.125	115.750
February 29	117.750	114.750	117.500
March 1	118.375	116.250	117.000
March 2	118.375	116.875	117.250
March 3	117.250	115.750	116.500
March 4	117.500	115.250	116.875
March 7	117.500	116.125	117.250
March 8	118.625	117.250	117.625
March 9	117.750	116.250	116.625
March 10	116.500	113.625	113.750
March 11	115.500	112.375	115.500
March 14	115.750	114.500	115.500
March 15	115.375	113.625	114.000
March 16	115.375	113.375	115.250
March 17	115.500	113.750	114.875
March 18	114.625	113.250	114.250
March 21	114.000	112.750	113.750
March 22	114.250	113.125	113.125
March 23	113.375	111.250	111.625
March 24	110.500	109.375	109.750
March 25	110.375	106.500	107.000

TECHNICAL ANALYSIS TIP—A telephoto-type effect can be produced by viewing monthly, weekly, and daily bar charts in combination. First, look at a bar chart plotting monthly data to gain a long-term perspective. Then, examine a bar chart of weekly data to determine the intermediate-term trend. Finally, a chart of daily data gives a short-term picture. Many technicians use this total picture to improve their probability of making profits by only making short-term trades in the direction of the intermediate and long-term trends.

Arithmetic versus Logarithmic Scale

The vertical price scale on a bar chart can be arithmetic or logarithmic. Each type has advantages and disadvantages. However, no consensus opinion exists among technicians as to which is best.

Figure 2–3
Daily Bar Chart

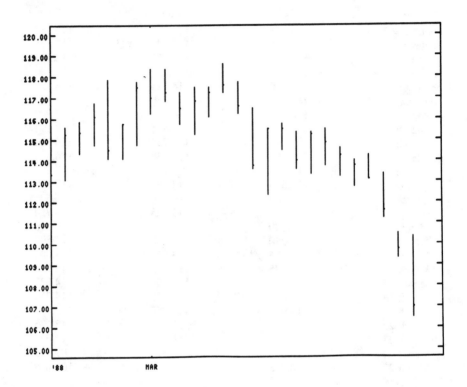

First, let's examine how the two scales differ. On an arithmetic scale, an equal distance for each price unit of change is shown on the vertical scale. Thus, the distance between 10 and 20 on the vertical scale equals the distance between 20 to 30, 30 to 40, and so on. On a logarithmic scale, the distance between each price unit of change represents an equal percentage change. For example, the difference between 10 to 20 and 40 to 80 is the same because each represents a 100 percent increase.

Figure 2–5 shows a comparison of arithmetic and logarithmic scales. Since chart patterns appear much the same on both scales, the type of vertical scale you use is up to personal preference. For consistency, the arithmetic scale will be used on charts throughout the remainder of this course.

Figure 2–4
Weekly Bar Chart

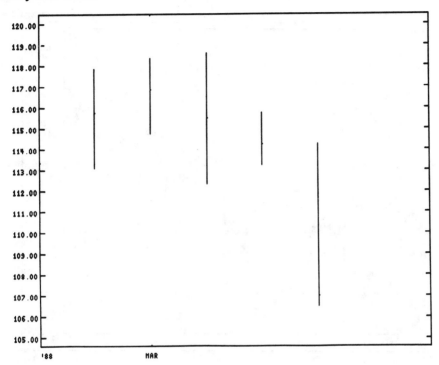

Volume

The volume of trading activity for each time period is normally shown at the bottom of a standard bar chart. Each period's (day's, week's, etc.) volume is recorded by a vertical bar directly below that period's price bar.

The higher the bar, the higher the volume for that period of time as illustrated in Figure 2–6. A vertical scale can be used along the bottom of the chart to help plot the data.

The significance of rising and declining volume relative to various price movements will be discussed in detail throughout this course.

Figure 2–5
Comparison of Arithmetic (Top) and Logarithmic (Bottom) Scales

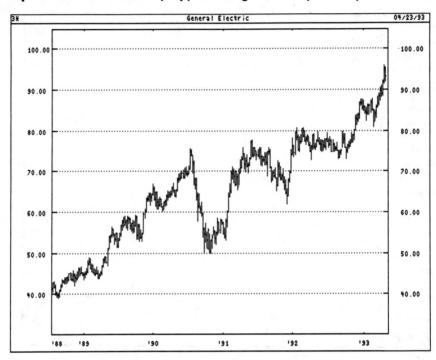

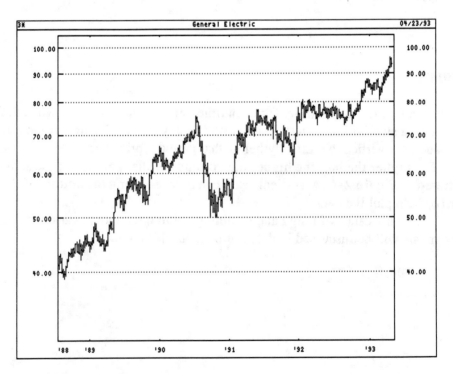

Open Interest

Open interest represents the total number of outstanding contracts for a particular commodity or futures contract. It is not applicable to stocks. Open interest is frequently plotted as a solid line along the bottom of the bar chart, usually just above the volume.

Where to Find Data

Although most of the data needed to prepare charts is readily available in the majority of daily newspapers, other sources do present more comprehensive information. For a list of recommended sources of technical related data, refer to the Appendix at the end of this course.

Chart Services

Preparing charts by hand is very time-consuming, especially if one is following many securities and calculating moving averages and other indicators for each security. One can easily spend half an hour each week updating just one chart.

Alternatively, technicians can purchase complete charts on a subscription basis at whatever frequency they want (weekly, bi-weekly, monthly, etc.). One must weigh the cost of the service against the time it takes to prepare charts to determine a service's benefit in each particular situation.

Those who do subscribe to a chart service typically will receive the charts through the mail, and they will only reflect data up to the time of mailing (which can be two to three days earlier). Space is often left for keeping current by updating the charts by hand until the next set of charts arrives.

TECHNICAL ANALYSIS TIP—If you are following a very limited number of securities, subscription to a chart service will be of less value to you than if you chart many securities or if you like to scan through charts looking for investment opportunities.

Figure 2–6
Example of Bar Chart with Volume Activity Plotted along the Bottom

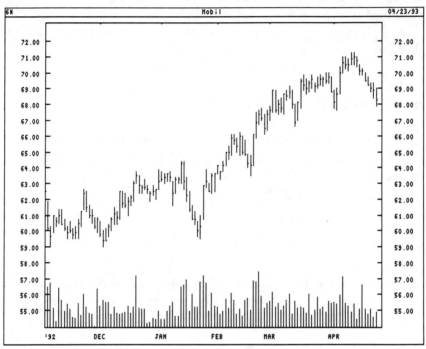

Personal Computer Software

Technical analysis software packages for use with personal computers are very popular and with good reason. Imagine that a technician wants to chart a stock's price for the last year — not just the closing price, but also the high and low. How much time will it take? Certainly more than an hour and even longer if all the stock prices are not at hand. Now imagine doing the same thing plus calculating and plotting various moving averages, oscillators, and other technical indicators in less than five minutes using technical analysis software.

Virtually all of the time-consuming tasks of preparing charts can be eliminated by using technical analysis software. In a matter of minutes, one can automatically retrieve the current and historical price and volume data from an on-line database and create a chart that might include a security's high-low price range, closing price, time frame (hours, days, weeks), volume, various moving averages, oscillators, and more. And, as opposed to subscribing to publications containing stock and commodity charts that are delivered through the mail (and, therefore, often contain information that is a couple of days old), these charts will always reflect current market conditions.

A number of features, working together, determine the overall effectiveness of a technical analysis software package. The type of data required, the source of data, and how one enters it into a package, for example, are significant factors in the type of analysis a technician can perform with a technical analysis software package. Some studies require specific data. To perform relative strength analysis to determine how a particular stock compares with the overall market, for example, a general standard of comparison is required, such as the Standard & Poor's 500 Index. If one can't get that data, the study can't be done.

Most technical analysis software packages require the input of vast quantities of data for plotting in charts. For instance, a basic high-low-close bar chart for a 90-day period requires 450 items of data. Although one can manually key in this data, most programs eliminate the trouble by accessing an on-line service, such as the Dow Jones News/Retrieval, from which one can download the required data. The time savings can be used, for example, to track more securities.

Charting capabilities are, of course, essential. A package that takes advantage of a personal computer's color graphics will make it easier to distinguish between securities and technical indicators when plotting more than one on a single chart. A technician might want to compare one or two stocks to an index or examine several technical indicators at the same time. The ability to display multiple charts on the screen in such cases is helpful.

Often a package comes close, but not close enough, to meeting analysis needs. If so, a feature allowing you to enter customized formulas for performing calculations on price data and for charting should be sought. This feature will permit fashioning a package to suit individual needs exactly.

Finally, it is likely that one will be preparing the same charts day after day. A package that has an autorun feature is a great time saver because it can be used to define a series of charts that will be prepared and printed automatically each day at the touch of a key.

TECHNICAL ANALYSIS TIP—Spend your time studying charts, not constructing and updating them. The cost of a personal computer software package or subscription to a chart service can be paid for many times over by a few good investments.

The vast majority of charts used throughout this course have been produced using technical analysis software and an IBM personal computer. Refer to the Appendix at the end of this course for a list of recommended technical analysis software packages.

True or False Quiz

Circle T if the statement is true or F if the statement is false.

T   F   1. A bar chart for a stock plots only its closing price and volume for each time period.

T   F   2. Monthly bar charts are frequently used to determine the short-term trend of stock prices.

T   F   3. On a bar chart, the horizontal tic to the right of the vertical bar (connecting high and low prices) represents the closing price for the period.

T   F   4. A weekly bar chart is a condensed version of a daily chart when the same price data is used.

T   F   5. When the vertical scale on a bar chart is logarithmic, the distances between 10 to 20 and 20 to 30 are equal.

T   F   6. Technical analysis software packages can be used to calculate and plot a variety of basic and advanced technical indicators quickly.

Answers

1. *False.* A bar chart for a stock plots high, low, and closing prices for each time period. In addition, volume is typically plotted at the bottom of the bar chart.

2. *False.* Monthly bar charts are normally used to gain a long-term perspective. Hourly or daily bar charts are often used to determine the short-term trend of stock prices.

3. *True.* See Figure 2–2.

4. *True.* See Figures 2–3 and 2–4 for an illustration.

5. *False.* On an arithmetic scale the distances between 10 to 20 and 20 to 30 are equal. On a logarithmic scale the distance between 20 to 30 is half as much as between 10 to 20 because it represents a 50 percent increase in price, while a 100 percent increases occurs from 10 to 20.

6. *True.*

PROFITABLE CHART PATTERNS

Major Reversal Chart Patterns

Market prices move in trends of varying duration and definition. While the trend is changing, identifiable chart patterns frequently develop. These patterns, known as *reversal chart patterns*, help identify when the market is changing direction, either from up to down or down to up. The primary importance of reversal patterns is that they help one sell securities before considerable price declines and cover short sales ahead of considerable advances.

Technicians have discovered many reversal chart patterns. Some occur frequently; others are rarely seen. Some are very reliable; others don't result in the price movements one would expect. This lesson presents a select group of reversal chart patterns, ones that have been proven to be of considerable validity over many years.

Before examining the characteristics of numerous reversal chart patterns, let's try to understand the forces behind a trend reversal. The forming of a market top and subsequent price reversal to the downside occurs as a result of supply overcoming demand (known as distribution). The opposite occurs at market bottoms when demand overcomes supply (known as accumulation). In both cases, this overcoming activity typically occurs gradually. Prices swing back and forth (in a manner that develops a reversal chart pattern) in a sideways fashion of some sort until a complete reversal is accomplished.

Keep in mind that the greater the time it takes for a reversal chart pattern to form, the more reliable the signal generated is, as well as the time horizon (short-, intermediate-, or long-term) forecasted by the signal. Over the years, technicians have found the following reversal chart patterns to be worth looking for:

1. Key reversals.
2. Head and shoulders tops and bottoms.
3. Rounding tops and bottoms (saucers).
4. Ascending and descending triangles.
5. Rectangles.
6. Double and triple tops and bottoms.
7. Diamond.
8. Rising and falling wedges.
9. V formations (spikes).

Let's examine each pattern in detail.

Key Reversals

Figure 3–1 illustrates a key reversal top. A key reversal bottom is shown in Figure 3–2.

Typical Price Action Key reversals occur during one period (usually one day) of market activity. A key reversal top is the result of prices quickly moving higher (to a new high in an uptrend) than the previous period's high, but closing near the lows of the day (and, at times, even lower than the previous period's low). Key reversal tops appear regularly in thinly traded stocks after an active advance.

The opposite occurs for a key reversal bottom. Prices first move sharply lower (to a new low in a downtrend) than the previous period's low and then move to the upside closing near the high for the day (and often higher than the previous period's high). A key reversal bottom is frequently called a *selling climax* as it often occurs at the end of a panic decline.

Typical Volume Action Key reversals normally are accompanied by unusually high volume.

Figure 3-1
Key Reversal Top

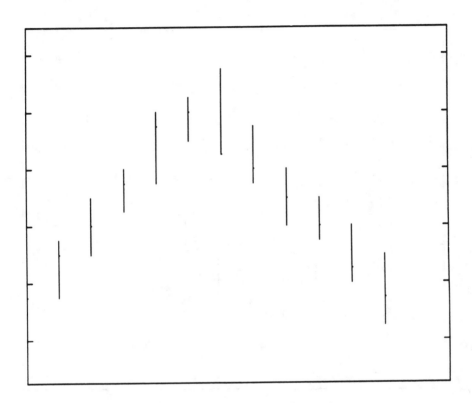

Frequency of Occurrence Key reversals appear often. They can develop in and of themselves or as a part of a larger chart pattern (such as the top of the head in a head and shoulders top formation).

Technical Significance A key reversal has only short-term (minor trend) significance. Its significance is, however, greatly enhanced if one or more of the following occurs:

1. The period's high penetrates the previous period's high significantly for a key reversal top or the period's low penetrates the previous period's low significantly for a key reversal bottom.
2. The key reversal period was preceded by a long, unbroken trend.

Figure 3–2
Key Reversal Bottom

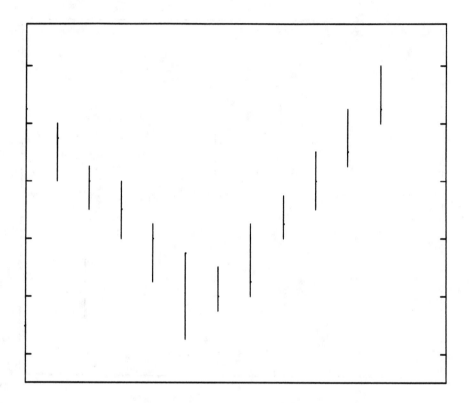

3. The period's closing price was below (for a key reversal top) or above (for a key reversal bottom) one or more immediately prior period ranges.

4. The period volume was particularly high.

Head and Shoulders Tops and Bottoms

A head and shoulders top is illustrated in Figure 3–3. Figure 3–4 shows a head and shoulders bottom.

Typical Price Action The head and shoulders top formation is one of the most common and most reliable chart patterns. It consists of a left shoulder, head, and right shoulder as shown in Figure 3–3. The left shoulder is typically formed at the end of an extensive advance. After prices drop from the peak of the left shoulder, they rally to a new high and then decline to near the low of the left shoulder to form the head part of the head and shoulders chart pattern. A final advance to a peak lower than that of the head followed by a decline in prices forms the right shoulder and completes the chart pattern.

A neckline can be drawn across the bottom of the left shoulder, head, and right shoulder. When the neckline is broken, you receive confirmation of a reversal in the trend. After moving lower, it is not uncommon for prices to pull back to the neckline before continuing their descent.

Head and shoulders bottoms are simply the inverse of head and shoulders tops. In some occasions, bottoms appear flatter than tops.

The majority of head and shoulder formations are not perfectly symmetrical. The neckline can be horizontal but often slopes up or down. However, for a head and shoulders top on an upsloping neckline, the lowest part of the

Figure 3–3
Head and Shoulders Top

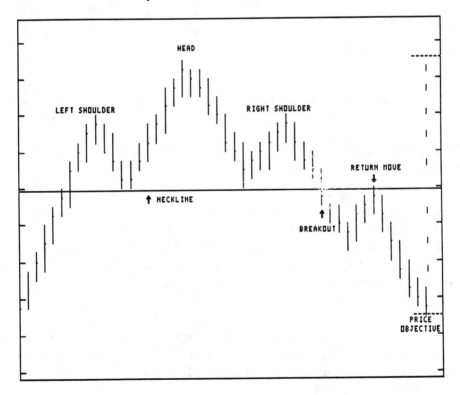

Figure 3–4
Head and Shoulders Bottom

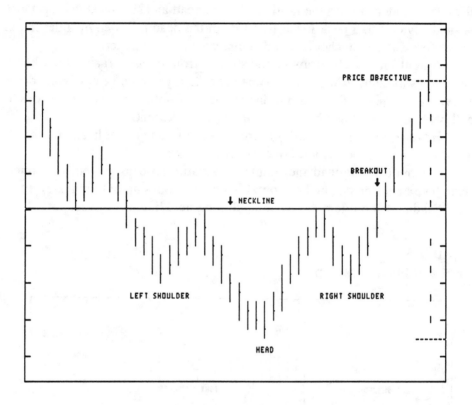

right shoulder should be appreciably lower than the top of the left shoulder. The inverse is true for head and shoulder bottoms.

Typical Volume Action For a head and shoulders top, volume is heavy on the rally portion of the left shoulder. Volume declines on the dip from the left shoulder peak and then again is heavy on the rally up to the top of the head. A reduction in volume occurs on the decline from the top of the head. The ensuing rally to create the right shoulder occurs on less volume than on previous rallies in this formation.

For a head and shoulders bottom, volume picks up on each rally with greater volume on the rally completing the right shoulder than on the rally completing the head. Between rallies, volume diminishes. If the neckline is broken on relatively low volume, it could be indicating a false signal, and a retest of lows may be forthcoming.

Frequency of Occurrence Head and shoulders chart patterns occur relatively frequently.

Technical Significance The minimum price objective after a head and shoulders neckline break is the same distance from the top of the head to the neckline. (The move prior to the head and shoulders pattern must be at least as great as the distance from the top of the head to the neckline.)

Rounding Tops and Bottoms (Saucers)

Rounding tops and bottoms, also known as *saucers*, are illustrated in Figures 3–5 and 3–6, respectively.

Figure 3–5
Rounding Top

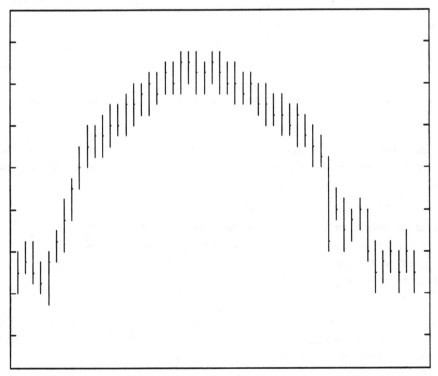

Figure 3–6
Rounding Bottom

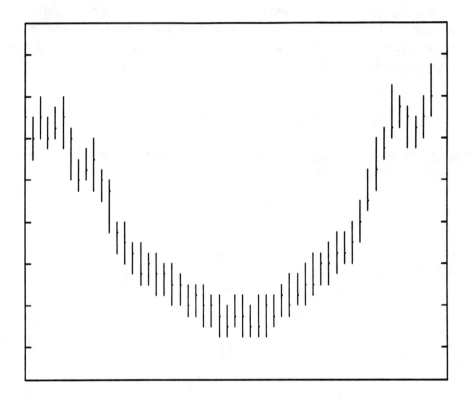

Typical Price Action Unlike many other reversal chart patterns, rounding tops and bottoms form as a result of a very gradual shift in supply and demand. A fairly symmetrical change in the direction of the trend occurs.

Typical Volume Action Volume declines throughout the first portion of the pattern (up to the top for a rounding top or bottom for a rounding bottom) and then rises on the decline in prices from the top (rounding top) or rally from the bottom (rounding bottom).

Frequency of Occurrence Rounding tops and bottoms are very rare, but do occur occasionally in interest sensitive and other securities where wide-swinging price fluctuations are unusual.

Technical Significance The significance of the rounding top and bottom patterns is simply to identify that a reversal in the trend has occurred. It implies no measured amount of movement in the new direction of the trend.

Ascending and Descending Triangles

Ascending and descending triangle chart patterns are illustrated in Figures 3–7 and 3–8, respectively.

Typical Price Action For an ascending triangle, prices swing between a horizontal top boundary line and an upward sloping bottom boundary line. An ascending triangle develops when demand is growing, but continues to meet supply at a certain price level. Once the supply is absorbed, prices break out of the pattern and move up rapidly.

Figure 3–7
Ascending Triangle

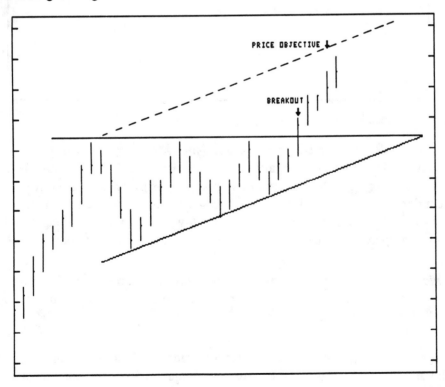

PRICE OBJECTIVE

BREAKOUT

Figure 3–8
Descending Triangle

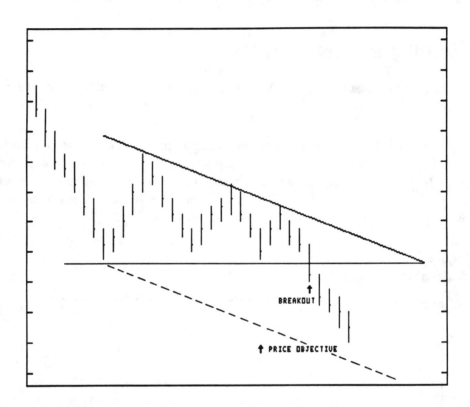

For a descending triangle, the opposite is true. Prices swing between a downward sloping top boundary line and a horizontal bottom boundary line. A descending triangle is formed when supply is growing, but continues to meet demand at a certain price level. Once the demand is exhausted, prices break out of the pattern and quickly move lower. Triangles are considered intermediate patterns, usually taking from one to three months to complete.

Typical Volume Action   Volume decreases as prices move toward the apex of either the ascending or descending triangle. Breakouts are accompanied by a marked increase in trading volume.

Frequency of Occurrence   Both ascending and descending triangles appear regularly on daily charts. They are less frequent, but still not unusual, on weekly charts.

Technical Significance Ascending and descending triangles offer excellent profit opportunities. The ascending triangle provides a bullish outlook, while the descending triangle suggests a bearish future.

Both types of triangles have similar measuring implications in regard to how far to expect prices to move after the breakout. Let's examine the measuring implication for an ascending triangle. It is illustrated in Figure 3–7.

First, a line is drawn parallel to the bottom boundary from the top of the first rally that initiated the pattern. This line will slope up and to the right. Prices will ordinarily move up until they reach this line.

The same measuring principle in inverse applies to descending triangles.

Rectangles

Examples of bullish and bearish rectangle chart patterns are provided in Figures 3–9 and 3–10, respectively.

Typical Price Action A rectangle pattern consists of sideways price movements that are contained within two horizontal (or near horizontal) lines at the top and the bottom. This area is also known as a *trading area* or *range*. Rectangles are formed when there is consistent supply of a security at a certain price and demand at a certain lower price. When the price reaches the lower price, the security is purchased, driving up the price until such time as it reaches the upper boundary and people are ready to sell and drive the price back to the lower boundary. This occurs repeatedly until one side or the other gives way and the pattern is broken.

A closing price outside the upper or lower boundary line implies the direction of the trend. If the closing price is above the upper boundary line, the probability is that prices will move higher. On the other hand, if the closing price is below the lower boundary line, prices will likely fall.

Typical Volume Action Volume action can give a clue as to whether the rectangle formation will ultimately be broken to the upside or downside. If volume is relatively higher on upward price swings than moves to the downside, it is likely the breakout will occur on the upside. On the other hand, if volume is relatively higher on downward price swings than moves to the upside, it is likely there will be a downside breakout of the rectangle.

Frequency of Occurrence Rectangles occur regularly and are easy to spot.

Figure 3–9
Bullish Rectangle

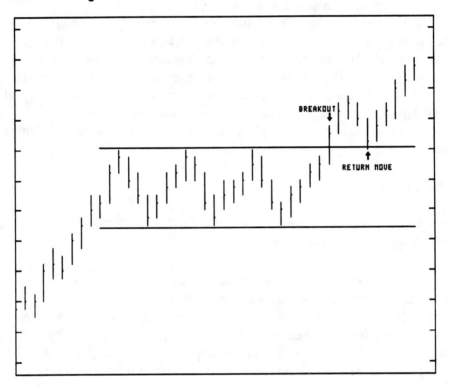

Technical Significance   A close above the upper boundary line or below the lower boundary line signals the direction of the trend. No measurement guidelines are established by rectangles for the distance prices will move in the direction of a breakout.

TECHNICAL ANALYSIS TIP — Some short-term traders make trades within well defined rectangles. They buy when prices reach the bottom boundary and sell short when prices reach the upper boundary. To protect themselves in the event of a pattern breakout, each time they buy or sell short, they also place stop-loss orders just outside the lower or upper boundary lines to minimize any potential losses. If the pattern is broken, they are stopped-out at a small loss, and they quickly place a new order in the direction of the breakout.

Figure 3–10
Bearish Rectangle

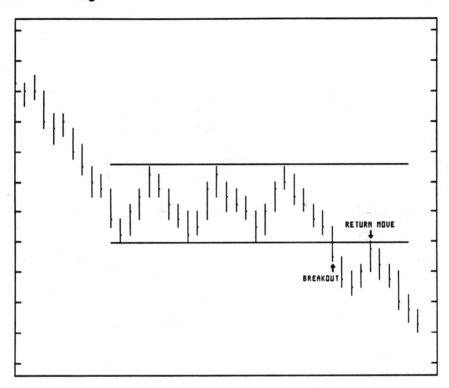

Double and Triple Tops and Bottoms

A double top and bottom chart pattern is illustrated in Figures 3–11 and 3–12, respectively. Examples of triple top and bottom chart patterns are shown in Figures 3–13 and 3–14, respectively.

Typical Price Action On a chart, a double top looks like the letter M. It forms when prices advance to a certain level, turn down, then rise again to near the previous peak, and then move down a second time to below the valley between the two peaks. The double bottom, which looks like the letter W, is the same as the double top except upside down. Triple tops and bottoms make three tops and bottoms, respectively, instead of two.

Figure 3–11
Double Top

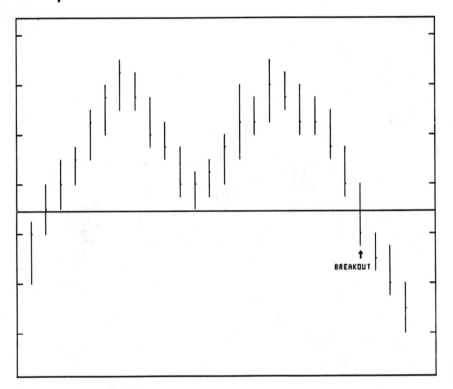

Typical Volume Action   For a double top, volume on the rise to the second peak is less than on the first peak. If volume is relatively higher, chances of a double top occurring are reduced. For a double bottom, volume shows a marked increase on the rally from the second bottom.

For triple tops, volume is relatively less on the second advance than the first and even less on the third advance. For triple bottoms, volume is relatively higher on the second rally than the first and still greater on the third advance.

Frequency of Occurrence   True double tops and bottoms are rare; triple tops and bottoms are even rarer.

Technical Significance   Double tops and bottoms are popular chart patterns, but are frequently mislabeled. In any uptrend, after a reaction, each new wave

Figure 3–12
Double Bottom

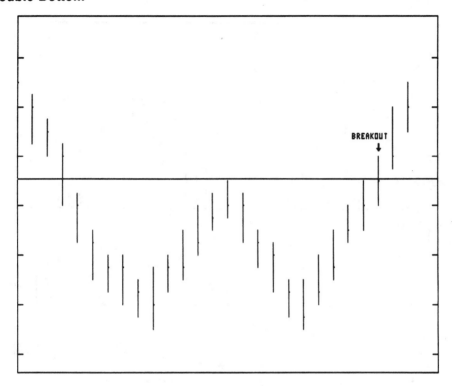

up will appear to be making a double top. However, the vast majority of the
time, prices carry to new highs and no double top is formed. One must wait
for confirmation of the pattern, which does not occur until the price goes
below the low price of the valley between the two peaks (or above the high
price of the peak between two valleys for double bottoms).

A further test of validity is the time element. Peaks should be separated
by a significant reaction. If the two tops (peaks) are near, they could very
well be part of a consolidation area. As a yardstick, use the criteria of peaks
being one month apart and the valley being at least 15 percent lower than the
top peak price.

True double and triple tops and bottoms do have measuring implications. Expect prices to move in the direction of the reversal at least the distance from the valley to the peak.

Figure 3–13
Triple Top

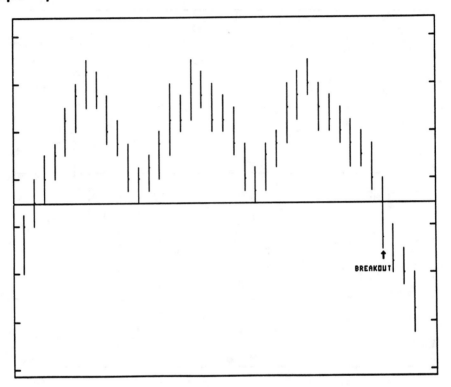

BREAKOUT

Diamond

The diamond formation derives its names from its pictorial resemblance on a chart to the diamond figure as illustrated in Figure 3–15.

Typical Price Action The diamond formation is actually the combination of two other chart patterns, namely the expanding triangle and the symmetrical triangle. During the expanding triangle part, price swings widen. Subsequently, price swings narrow during the symmetrical triangle part of the diamond formation. The formation is completed when one of the boundary lines forming the symmetrical triangle part of the diamond formation is broken.

The diamond formation can also occur in a fashion similar to a complex head and shoulders pattern with a V-shaped neckline. Although the diamond

Figure 3–14
Triple Bottom

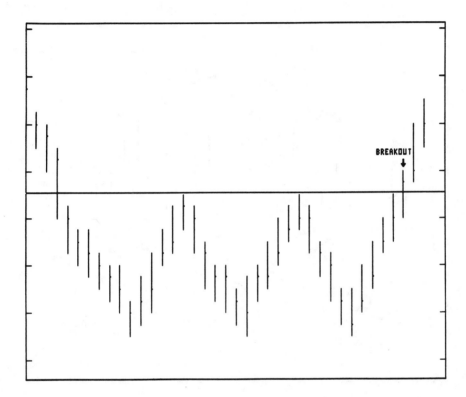

BREAKOUT

formation can turn out to be a continuation pattern, it usually is a reversal pattern.

Typical Volume Action Volume increases during the first half of the diamond formation (the part that looks like an expanding triangle) and declines gradually during the second half (the part that looks like a symmetrical triangle). Volume typically increases on the breakout from the diamond formation.

Frequency of Occurrence The diamond formation is seen rarely. It normally appears at market tops and not at market bottoms, since it requires a relatively active (high volume) environment to develop.

Figure 3–15
Diamond Formation

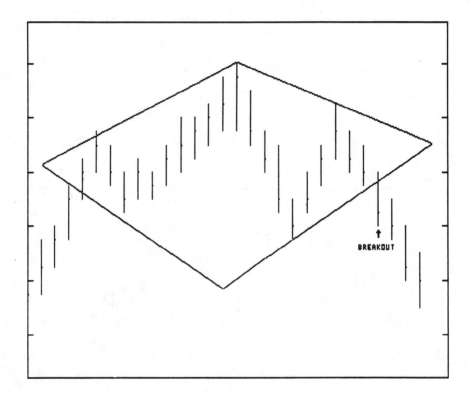

BREAKOUT

Technical Significance On a breakout of the diamond formation, prices should move a minimum amount equal to the distance from the top to the bottom of the pattern. Generally, prices move farther than the minimum measurement.

Rising and Falling Wedges

Figures 3–16 and 3–17 illustrate rising and falling wedge chart patterns, respectively.

Typical Price Action Wedges are characterized by prices fluctuating between two converging boundary lines. For a rising wedge, the boundary lines are slanted upward with the lower line being at a steeper angle than the upper

Figure 3–16
Rising Wedge

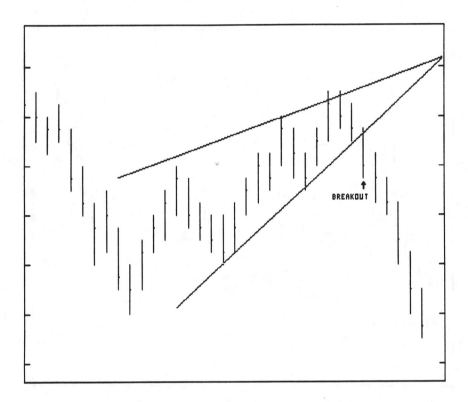

line. For a falling wedge, the boundary lines are slanted down and the upper line is at a steeper angle than the lower line. Breakouts normally occur at least two-thirds of the way to the apex of the converging boundary lines.

On a daily chart, a wedge formation typically takes three or more weeks to complete.

Typical Volume Action Trading volume in a wedge gradually diminishes as prices move toward the apex of the wedge and then rises on the breakout.

Frequency of Occurrence Wedges are formed on a regular basis.

Technical Significance The rising wedge implies a situation that is growing weaker from a technical perspective. When prices break through the lower

Figure 3–17
Falling Wedge

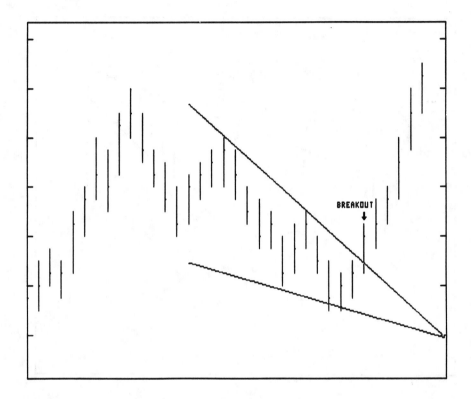

line of a rising wedge, they usually fall in earnest. Sell signals generated by breakouts below the lower line of rising wedges are more reliable in bear markets than in bull markets.

The falling wedge typifies a situation that is getting stronger from a technical perspective. When prices break through the upper boundary of a falling wedge, they tend to move sideways for a period of time before beginning to rise.

V Formations (Spikes)

Contrary to most reversal patterns which gradually change direction, the V formation (otherwise known as a spike) suddenly reverses the trend with little warning. Examples of a V formation top and bottom are provided in Figures 3–18 and 3–19.

Typical Price Action   Prices move quickly either up or down and move beyond expectations. Prices become overextended and snap back quickly without warning.

Typical Volume Action   Volume is relatively heavy throughout the pattern.

Frequency of Occurrence   V formations develop regularly, particularly in volatile, popular stocks.

Figure 3–18
V Top

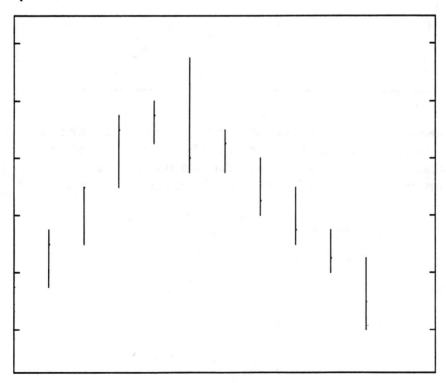

Figure 3–19
V Bottom

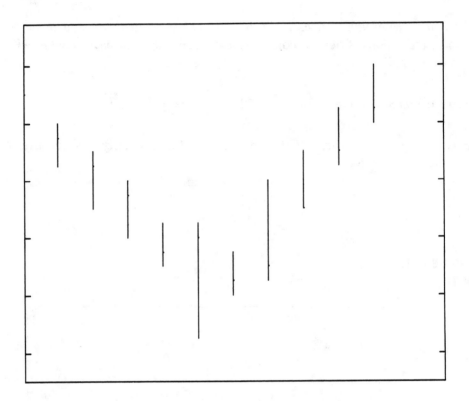

Technical Significance V formations occur so quickly and with such little warning that the pattern can be spotted only after the fact and only after a significant move in the opposite direction has already occurred. Thus, profit opportunities are limited with regard to V formation chart patterns.

True or False Quiz

Circle T if the statement is true or F if the statement is false.

T   F   1. A reversal at a market top occurs as a result of the process of demand overcoming supply (accumulation).

T   F   2. The greater the time it takes for a reversal chart pattern to form, the more reliable the signal generated is.

T   F   3. Key reversals usually occur during one day of market activity.

T   F   4. During a head and shoulders top chart pattern, volume increases on each successive rally.

T   F   5. Confirmation of a reversal in trend is received when the neckline of a head and shoulders chart top or bottom is broken.

T   F   6. Similar to many other reversal chart patterns, rounding tops and bottoms result from a very gradual shift in supply and demand.

T   F   7. Ascending and descending triangles occur with such little warning that you can spot the patterns only after the fact. Profit opportunities are limited with regard to ascending and descending triangles.

T   F   8. A double top looks like the letter M.

T   F   9. The diamond formation is seen frequently at market bottoms.

T   F   10. Wedge chart patterns form when prices fluctuate between two converging boundary lines.

Refer to Charts 3A through 3D to answer questions 11 to 14.

T   F   11. The chart below shows a rounding top chart pattern.

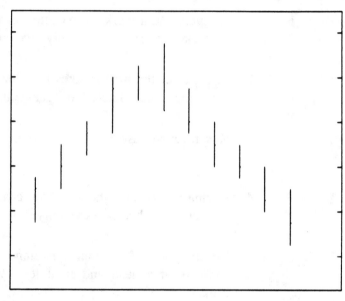

T   F   12. When prices break through the neckline of the head and shoulders bottom pattern shown in the following chart, it is likely that they will rise to at least $13¾.

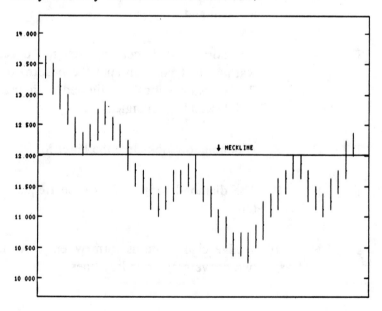

T   F   13. The chart below illustrates a bullish rectangle formation.

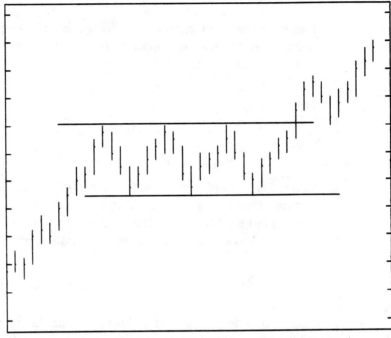

T   F   14. The rally from point A in the following chart would likely occur on expanding volume.

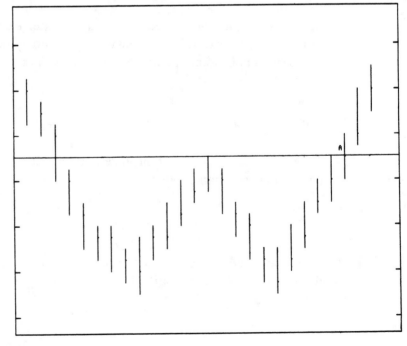

Answers

1. *False.* Demand overcomes supply (accumulation) forming market bottoms. A reversal at a market top occurs when supply overcomes demand (distribution).

2. *True.*

3. *True.*

4. *False.* For a head and shoulders top, volume is heavy on the rally portion of the left shoulder. Volume is again heavy on the rally to the top of the head. However, the final rally to create the right shoulder occurs on less volume than on previous rallies in this formation.

5. *True.*

6. *False.* Rounding tops and bottoms are unlike many other reversal chart patterns that form from a much quicker shift in supply and demand.

7. *False.* Ascending and descending triangles offer excellent profit opportunities. They are relatively easy to spot as they develop and have measuring implications in regard to how far prices are expected to move after a breakout.

8. *True.*

9. *False.* The diamond formation is seen rarely. It normally appears at market tops, not market bottoms.

10. *True.*

11. *False.* Chart 3A reflects a key reversal top. See Figure 3–5 for an illustration of a rounding top.

12. *True.* It is probable that prices will move a distance away from the neckline equal to that from the top of the head to the neckline.

13. *True.*

14. *True.* Refer to the section on the double bottom chart pattern.

Consolidation Formations

Consolidation formations occur when security prices move up or down too fast and reach a level at which the demand or supply that produced the move is completely absorbed. At that point three things can occur. First, prices can reverse their trend, in which case you would likely see a reversal pattern develop. Second, prices can decline or rise to a support level before building up steam again. Third, prices can move sideways, creating a consolidation formation from which to base a further move in the direction of the trend.

In essence a consolidation formation can be defined as a sideways price movement that temporarily interrupts an up or down move in prices. There are many consolidation formations. This lesson will teach four of the most reliable ones, namely flags, pennants, head and shoulders continuation patterns, and symmetrical triangles.

Flags

A flag pattern in an uptrend is illustrated in Figure 4–1.

Typical Price Action A flag pattern, as one would expect, looks like a flag on a chart. It represents a pause in a quick, almost vertical, up or down move in prices. Prices move sideways forming a flag-like pattern, break out from that pattern, and then continue in the same direction as before.

Figure 4–1
Flag

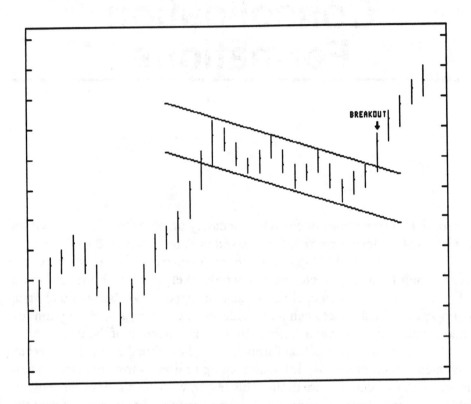

Typical Volume Action Volume is extremely heavy before the flag formation begins. As the pattern develops, volume diminishes to a relatively low level. Finally, volume explodes as prices complete and break out of the flag pattern.

Frequency of Occurrence Flags appear regularly on daily charts, but because of the short time they take to develop (typically less than four weeks), they are rarely seen on weekly charts and are nonexistent on monthly charts.

Technical Significance Flags typically appear at the halfway point of an up or down move. Therefore, one can expect prices to move about the same distance after the breakout from the flag pattern as they did just prior to the pattern.

Pennants

Figure 4–2 illustrates a pennant chart pattern that occurs in an uptrend.

Typical Price Action Pennants and flags have the same characteristics except that a pennant is formed by converging, rather than parallel boundary lines. Pennants slant down in uptrends and up in downtrends. As with flags, pennant consolidations are characteristic of fast up and down moves in prices.

Typical Volume Action Volume is extremely heavy before the pennant formation begins. As the pattern develops, volume diminishes to a relatively low level. Finally, volume increases significantly as prices complete and break out of the pennant pattern.

**Figure 4–2
Pennant**

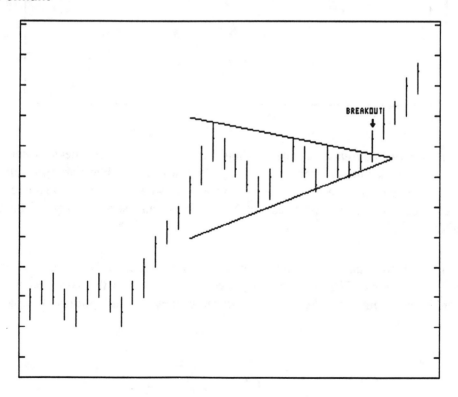

Figure 4–3
Bullish Head and Shoulders Continuation Pattern

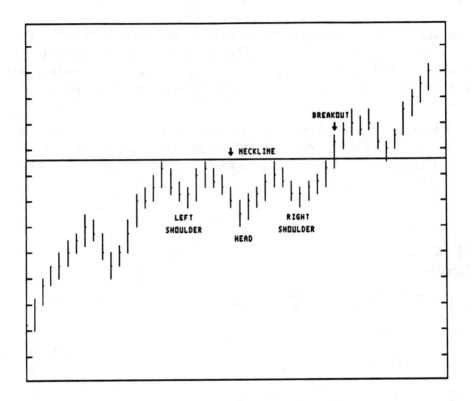

Frequency of Occurence Pennants should take less than four weeks to complete and break out. Therefore, like flags, they are more identifiable in daily charts than weekly charts and never appear on monthly charts. They occur most frequently in the last phase of bull markets and second stage of bear markets.

Technical Significance Pennants typically appear about midway through an up or down move. Therefore, expect prices to move about the same distance after the breakout from the pennant pattern as they did just prior to the pattern.

Figure 4–4
Bearish Head and Shoulders Continuation Pattern

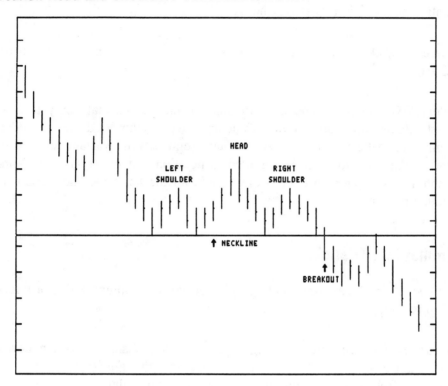

Head and Shoulders Continuation Patterns

Bullish and bearish head and shoulders continuation patterns are illustrated in Figures 4–3 and 4–4, respectively.

Typical Price Action   Head and shoulders continuation patterns are inverted relative to the direction of the price trend before their appearance. When prices are trending lower, a head and shoulders continuation pattern appears similar to a head and shoulders top. (Refer to Lesson 3 for a complete description of head and shoulders tops and bottoms.) In an uptrend, a head and shoulders continuation pattern appears like a head and shoulders bottom.

Typical Volume Action   For the head and shoulders continuation pattern, volume decreases instead of increasing (as with the head and shoulders top) on the left shoulder and head, as well as the right shoulder. Volume does resemble that of head and shoulders tops and bottoms on breakout from the continuation patterns; it is relatively heavy.

Frequency of Occurence   Head and shoulders continuation patterns occur occasionally.

Technical Significance   The measurement characteristics that apply to head and shoulders tops and bottoms sometimes work with head and shoulders continuation patterns, but not with enough regularity to warrant reliance on them. Technical significance is limited to notation that prices are continuing an uptrend or downtrend upon a breakout from the head and shoulders continuation pattern.

Symmetrical Triangle

An illustration of a symmetrical triangle formation in an uptrend is provided in Figure 4–5.

Typical Price Action   Prices swing in a narrowing fashion between down-slanting upper and upslanting lower boundary lines that are fairly symmetrical in nature. There must be a minimum of four reversal points in the triangle. A breakout can occur at any time between two-thirds of the way to the apex and the apex.

Typical Volume Action   Volume diminishes as prices approach the apex of the triangle. On a valid upside breakout, volume is heavy; on a valid downside breakout, volume is often light at first and then picks up significantly after a few days.

Beware of upside breakouts on light volume and downside breakouts accompanied by heavy volume. They could be a warning of false moves.

Frequency of Occurrence   Symmetrical triangles appear regularly on price charts.

Technical Significance   On a valid upside breakout, you can expect prices to continue upward until they reach a line drawn parallel to the lower boundary line. The opposite is true for a valid downside breakout.

Figure 4–5
Symmetrical Triangle

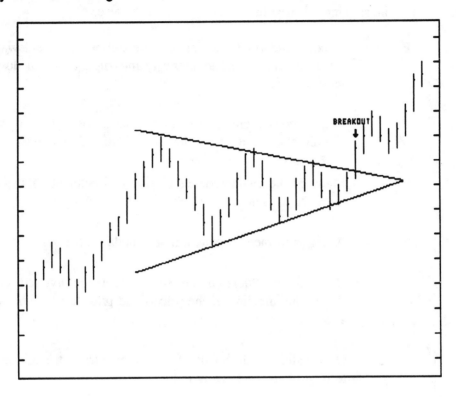

True or False Quiz

Circle T if the statement is true or F if the statement is false.

T   F   1. A consolidation formation can be defined as a sideways price movement that temporarily interrupts an up or down move in prices.

T   F   2. After a consolidation formation, prices move in the opposite direction than before the consolidation formation.

T   F   3. Many of the characteristics of flag and pennant chart patterns are the same.

T   F   4. A flag is formed by converging boundary lines.

T   F   5. Head and shoulders continuation patterns are inverted relative to the direction of the price trend prior to their appearance.

T   F   6. On a valid upside breakout of a symmetrical triangle pattern, volume is relatively light.

Answers

1. *True.*

2. *False.* A consolidation formation "temporarily interrupts" an up or down move in prices. Prices continue in the same direction upon a breakout from a consolidation formation.

3. *True.*

4. *False.* A flag is formed by parallel boundary lines as illustrated in Figure 4–1. A pennant is formed by converging boundary lines as illustrated in Figure 4–2.

5. *True.*

6. *False.* Volume is relatively heavy on a valid upside breakout of a symmetrical triangle pattern.

LESSON 5

Gaps

In addition to reversal and consolidation formations, a group of chart patterns based on gaps in price activity appear on charts.

A *gap* represents a price range on a chart at which no trading takes place (no shares trade hands). Gaps can appear in an uptrend (as shown in Figure 5–1) signifying market strength or a downtrend (as shown in Figure 5–2) suggesting market weakness. When a gap occurs in an uptrend, the current period's low is higher than the previous period's high. In a downtrend, a gap appears when the current period's high is lower than the previous period's low.

Frequency of Appearance

Gaps occur more frequently on charts covering short time frames (such as hourly or daily) than they do on longer term charts (such as those plotting weekly or monthly data). However, they are of greater significance on long-term charts than short-term charts. The reason for that is easily explained.

Gaps are common on daily charts because they can be created on a daily basis (20 or more times during a month). At the end of each day, an opportunity exists that the current day's high (or low) price will be lower than (or higher than) any price at which that stock trades on the next day. However, on a monthly chart, only one opportunity each month exists for a gap to occur. It is rare, and thus of great significance, that the high (or low) price for the current month will not be crossed at some time during the next month and create a gap. About the only time gaps occur on monthly charts is when a panic rise or decline occurs at the end of the month.

Figure 5–1
Gap in an Uptrend

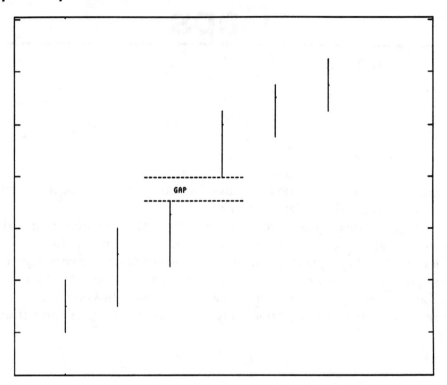

Insignificant Gaps

Some gaps are significant while others are meaningless. Gaps that are not significant include:

1. A gap caused by a stock trading an amount equal to the minimum permitted change in price. For example, most stocks trade at intervals of an eighth of a point. If a stock closed at its high for the day at $10 per share and then opened the next day at $10\frac{1}{8} per share (and traded at or above the opening price for the remainder of that day), the gap created is of no technical significance.

2. For higher-priced stocks, the spread between successive bids is frequently $\frac{1}{4}$ or $\frac{1}{2}$ point. Gaps equal to the normal interval between successive bids are of no technical significance.

Figure 5–2
Gap in a Downtrend

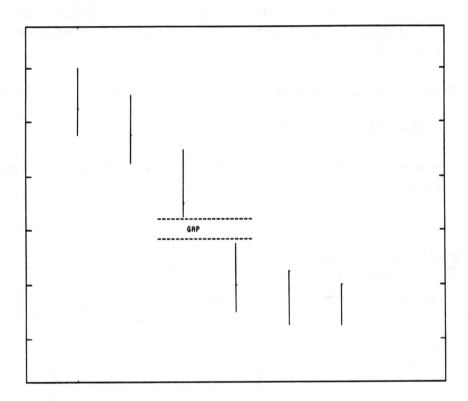

3. For medium to high-priced issues that have low trading volume, gaps are regular and numerous. They are also not significant.

4. Ex-dividend gaps frequently occur when a company pays a dividend. They are actually an alteration to the book value of an issue and have no trend implications.

Significant Gaps

Four types of gaps regularly occur on charts. One type (common) is of less significance than the other three types (breakaway, runaway, and exhaustion). An example and discussion highlighting the characteristics of each type of gap follows.

COMMON GAP

The common gap is the least important gap. It normally occurs in thinly traded markets or within a trading area or price congestion pattern. It often merely reflects a lack of trading interest. Three common gaps are illustrated in Figure 5–3.

Typical Price Action   A stock moves in a certain price range, say $15 to $25 per share. A gap is then created by a jump from $22 to $25. It is likely that congestion will be formed between $22 and $25.

Typical Volume Action   Volume is relatively low due to being in a congestion pattern.

Figure 5–3
Common Gaps

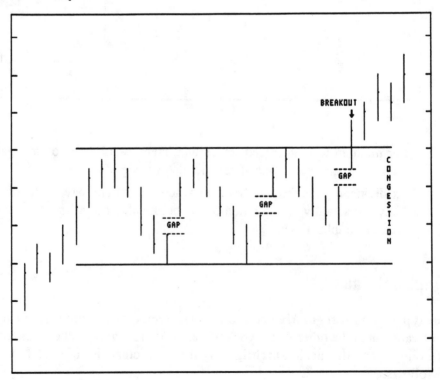

Frequency of Occurrence Common gaps occur often as the name "common" suggests.

Technical Significance Common gaps are of little forecasting significance. However, they can alert technicians to a congestion pattern that is in the process of being constructed.

BREAKAWAY GAP

Most breakouts from a horizontal price boundary are attended by a breakaway gap. An example is provided in Figure 5–4.

Typical Price Action A breakaway gap occurs on a price breakout through a horizontal pattern boundary. Typically, the horizontal pattern boundary is part of a price congestion pattern (such as an ascending triangle) and the breakout marks its completion. For example, suppose a stock has traded up to $21 per share, stopped, and turned lower over and over. This would suggest both a persistent demand for and a large supply of stock available for sale at the $21 level. Current stock holders observe the price action and make their stock available at the $21 level or figure that once the stock breaks the $21 barrier, it will go much higher. (Therefore, they hold their stock for the time being.) This creates a vacuum so that once the supply of stock at $21 is absorbed, the next buyer finds none available at $21⅛, $21¼, etc. He or she must bid higher and thus create a breakaway gap.

Typical Volume Action Volume is normally heavy when a breakaway gap occurs. If volume is higher before the gap than after, chances are about 50–50 that the gap will be filled on the next minor reaction. If volume is higher after the gap than before, chances are slim that near-term reactions will fill the gap.

TECHNICAL ANALYSIS TIP — Almost every legitimate breakout from a price congestion formation is accompanied by a breakaway gap. Although not all breakaway gaps appear on charts (because they occur during the day and not between one day's closing price and the following day's opening price), beware of breakouts not accompanied by gaps. Gaps seldom occur in false breakouts (those which do not follow through in the direction of the breakout).

Figure 5–4
Breakaway Gap

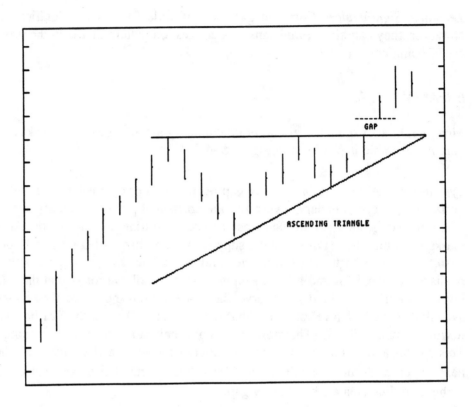

Frequency of Occurrence   Breakaway gaps appear much less frequently than common gaps, but often enough to warrant watching for them.

Technical Significance   Breakaway gaps are highly significant. They often signal the start of a rapid price move in the direction of the breakout. In the case of an upward move, this is due to buying demand that is stronger than selling pressure, often resulting in prices moving up quickly until balance is restored between supply and demand. The opposite is true for down movements.

RUNAWAY GAP

The runaway gap is a reliable indicator of a strong underlying trend. It is sometimes called a *continuation* or *measuring gap*. An example of a runaway gap is provided in Figure 5–5.

Typical Price Action   Runaway gaps occur in the middle of fast up or down price movements. This is typically when price quotes are moving rapidly and easily relative to the volume of transactions.

Typical Volume Action   Runaway gaps typically occur on moderate volume when the price is seemingly moving effortlessly. At times, runaway gaps are accompanied by relatively high volume, which increases the probability of a strong underlying trend in the direction of the move.

Figure 5–5
Runaway Gap

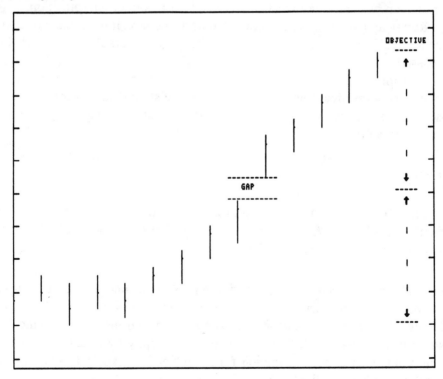

TECHNICAL ANALYSIS TIP—Runaway gaps frequently occur about half-way through an up or down price move. Therefore, you can expect that prices will move about the same percentage amount from the gap to the end of the move (a congestion or reversal pattern) as it has from the beginning of the move to the gap. Since it is the same "percentage" move, the vertical distance on a chart is about equal on a logarithmic scaled chart. On a chart with an arithmetic vertical scale, the advance will be greater (after the gap) than the vertical distance (before the gap) on a chart; declines will be less.

Frequency of Occurrence Runaway gaps occur less often than common or breakaway gaps but are more significant from a technical perspective.

Technical Significance Runaway gaps are a sign of significant strength in an uptrend or weakness in a downtrend. They are easy to distinguish from common or breakaway gaps. Distinguishing a runaway gap from an exhaustion gap is not easy initially. However, the price and volume action on the day after the gap provides the evidence you need for a correct interpretation.

Runaway gaps usually are not filled until the next intermediate or major price move. This typically occurs only after a considerable amount of time has passed.

Multiple runaway gaps can occur. When two or more such gaps occur, the measuring implications are less certain. One should act conservatively in these situations, recognizing that each additional runaway gap brings nearer a price top or bottom.

EXHAUSTION GAP

An exhaustion gap is the last gasp of an up or down price move. It is very difficult to distinguish from a runaway gap until after the fact. An exhaustion gap is illustrated in Figure 5–6.

Typical Price Movement An exhaustion gap is associated with a quick up or down movement in price (like a runaway gap). Prices move rapidly until, suddenly, they meet an abundance of supply in an up move or demand in a down move. At that point, the move is ended abruptly by a day of very high trading volume. It is not uncommon for an exhaustion gap to appear between the next to the last and the last day of a move.

Figure 5–6
Exhaustion Gap

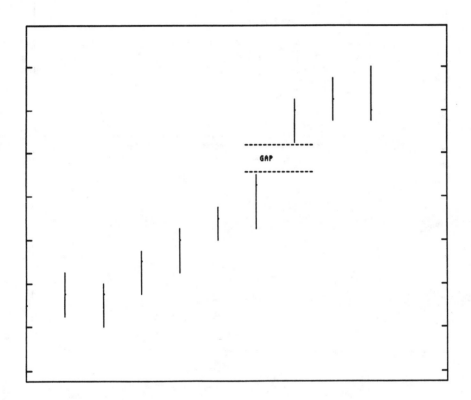

Typical Volume Activity An exhaustion gap is usually accompanied by a day of very high volume on a relative basis.

Frequency of Occurrence By their nature, exhaustion gaps occur with low frequency at the end of up or down price moves.

Technical Significance An exhaustion gap implies the end of an up or down move. After an exhaustion gap, you can expect an area pattern to form that eventually leads to price continuation or reversal. Even if price does eventually continue in the direction it was moving prior to the exhaustion gap, anticipate a time delay in the price advance or decline (that may warrant closing out your positions, depending on your investment time horizon). On the day following a gap, if a reversal day develops with the closing prices back to near the edge of the gap, it is extremely probable that the gap is an exhaustion

Figure 5–7
Island Reversal

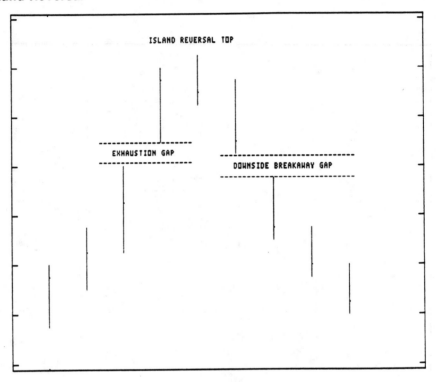

rather than a runaway gap. Exhaustion gaps are normally filled in two to five days.

TECHNICAL ANALYSIS TIP—Exhaustion and runaway gaps have similar characteristics that make them difficult to distinguish from each other initially. When one of these gaps occurs, immediately place protective stop-loss orders close to the gap price. Even if you think it will be an exhaustion gap, you do not need to immediately sell your positions (or cover short positions) or reverse your positions. You can wait until more evidence is present.

Figure 5–8
Progression of Gaps

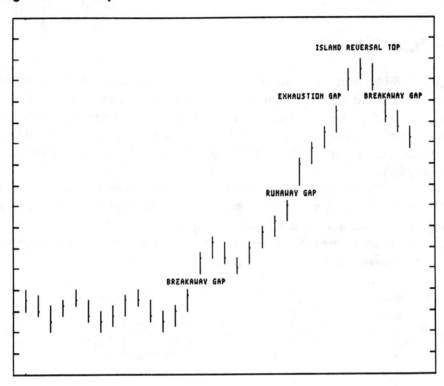

The Island Reversal

Occasionally, a section of a chart is isolated from the rest of the chart by gaps appearing at approximately the same horizontal price level. When this pattern occurs, it is known as an *island reversal*. Typically, the gap leading to the island reversal is an exhaustion gap, and the gap completing the island reversal pattern is a breakaway gap as illustrated in Figure 5–7.

An island reversal can represent one or more periods of trading activity. It can also be part of another chart pattern (such as the head of a head and shoulders pattern). It is characterized by relatively high volume.

By itself, an island reversal does not suggest that a long-term top or bottom has occurred. However, prices do frequently retrace the minor move that preceded it. Much of that retracement is accomplished by the time an island reversal is charted, thereby minimizing the value of any trading opportunity.

The Total Picture

Figure 5–8 illustrates a progression of gap occurrences (excluding common gaps which could occur throughout). An upward breakaway gap typically releases prices from a congestion pattern. A runaway gap increases the upward momentum. An exhaustion gap signals an approaching top that could be an island reversal. Finally, a downside breakaway gap starts things in the opposite direction.

Typically, the gaps would not appear in as orderly a fashion as illustrated in Figure 5–8. Gaps could appear in any combination of order. For example, you could have multiple breakaway gaps and no runaway gaps in a particular up movement. Nonetheless, the significance of each type of gap remains as summarized in the following table:

Type of Gap	Significance	Signals
Common	Little	—
Breakaway	Great	Significant market move
Runaway	Great	Halfway point of a price movement
Exhaustion	Great	Very bearish or very bullish

A Wall Street Myth—Gaps Must Be Closed

When a gap occurs on a price chart, it is not uncommon to read or hear someone say that the price must come back and fill the gap that was created. Over time, the probability is that the gap will be filled, since most securities trade in certain price ranges. However, there is absolutely no reason why it *must* be closed. And, frequently, when it is closed, it is only after the price has moved far away from the gap.

For example, over a period of time, a stock moves in a range from $9 to $15 per share. One day it closes at the top of the range. The next day it opens at $15½ and continues to move up from there, causing a gap to occur. The price subsequently climbs to $25 before retreating back through $15 ½ closing the gap. The gap is closed, but only after a period of time (which could be months or years) has passed. Basing an investment decision on "gaps must be closed" is not sound investing.

True or False Quiz

Circle T if the statement is true or F if the statement is false.

T   F   1. Gaps in an uptrend signify market weakness.

T   F   2. Gaps occur more frequently on monthly charts than on daily charts.

T   F   3. Gaps appearing on weekly charts are more significant than those on daily charts.

T   F   4. Ex-dividend gaps have bearish trend implications.

T   F   5. The four types of gaps that regularly occur on charts are called common, breakaway, runaway, and exhaustion.

T   F   6. A common gap often occurs on a breakout from a price congestion area on a chart.

T   F   7. Runaway gaps are not immediately distinguishable from exhaustion gaps.

T   F   8. A breakaway gap frequently occurs about halfway through an up or down price move.

T   F   9. By itself, an island reversal signals a major top or bottom has occured.

T   F   10. Gaps are always closed.

Refer to the following chart to answer questions 11 to 14.

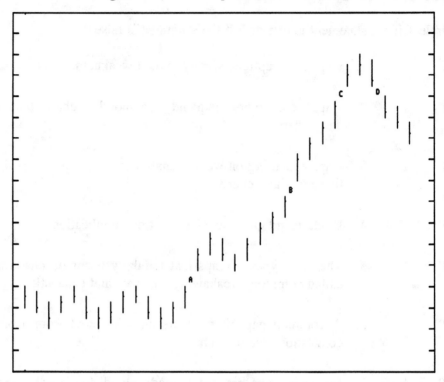

T   F   11. The gap labelled A on the chart is a common gap.

T   F   12. The gap labelled A on the chart usually occurs on relatively heavy volume.

T   F   13. The gap labelled B on the chart is a runaway gap.

T   F   14. The gap labelled C on the chart is an exhaustion gap that is of little technical significance.

Answers

1. *False.* Gaps in an uptrend signify market strength.

2. *False.* Gaps appear more often on shorter-term daily charts than on longer-term monthly charts, since they have 20 or more times as many opportunities per month to form.

3. *True.* The longer the period of time covered by each bar on a bar chart, the more significant gaps become. Therefore, a gap on a weekly chart is of greater technical significance than a gap on a daily chart.

4. *False.* Ex-dividend gaps have no trend implications.

5. *True.*

6. *False.* A breakaway gap often occurs on a breakout from a price congestion area on a price chart. Common gaps normally appear within a trading area or price congestion pattern.

7. *True.* You must analyze price and volume action on the day(s) following the gap to determine whether it is a runaway or exhaustion gap.

8. *False.* A runaway gap, not a breakaway gap, frequently occurs about halfway through an up or down price move.

9. *False.* An island reversal signals a major top or bottom only when it is part of another reversal pattern, such as a head and shoulders top or bottom.

10. *False.* Most gaps are closed over time, but not all.

11. *False.* The gap labelled A on the chart is a breakaway gap.

12. *True.*

13. *True.*

14. *False.* The gap labelled C on the chart is an exhaustion gap. However, it is of great technical significance as it implies the end of an up or down price move.

KEY ANALYTICAL
TOOLS

Trendlines and Channels

As shown in Lesson 1, one of the principles that technical analysis is based on is that prices move in trends. These trends can be up, down, or sideways as illustrated in Figure 6–1. An uptrend is characterized by successively higher highs and higher lows. A downtrend occurs on successively lower highs and lower lows. A sideways trend reflects horizontal price movement.

Trends can be brief or of long duration. They are typically classified as short-, intermediate-, or long-term. Although there are no generally accepted definitions of these three terms, short-term roughly refers to the next three months; intermediate-term is about three to six months from the present time; and long-term is considered to be approximately six months to one year from the current period.

Investors try to determine when prices are in an uptrend or downtrend. They profit by determining the trend and then following it until it is reversed. Of the many charting tools available, the trendline is most widely used by technicians to identify trends and trend reversals.

How Trendlines Are Drawn

Drawing trendlines is easy. A trendline is simply a straight line that connects a series of security prices, either tops or bottoms.

An up trendline is a straight line that connects a series of reaction lows, as illustrated in Figure 6–2. Note that the trendline appears at the bottom of the price pattern and is drawn up and to the right.

Figure 6–1
Uptrend (Top), Downtrend (Middle), and Sideways Trend (Bottom)

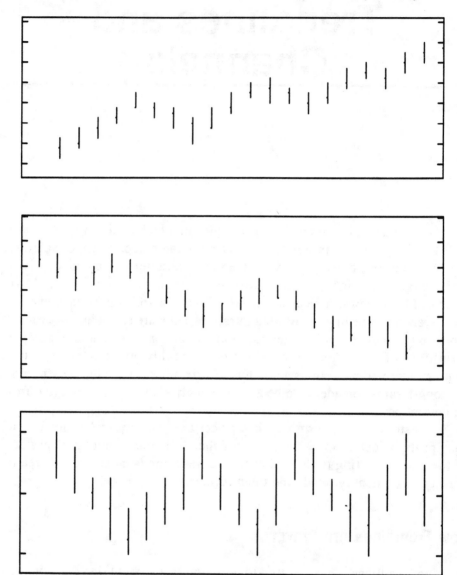

Figure 6–2
Up Trendline

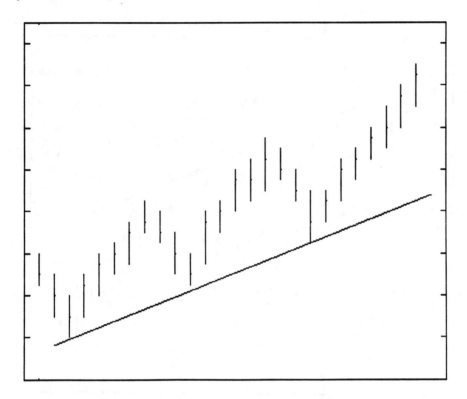

A down trendline is a straight line that connects a series of rally tops, as illustrated in Figure 6–3. Note that, in this case, the trendline is at the top of the price pattern. It is drawn down and to the right.

Some guidelines to use when drawing trendlines are appropriate. First of all, there must be at least two tops or bottoms to begin a trendline. This only makes sense, because one must have two points in order to draw a straight line. Second, after drawing a trendline based on two tops or bottoms, one will frequently find that a higher top or lower bottom has been made, requiring the trendline to be redrawn.

Significance of a Trendline

The significance of a trendline is determined by two factors, namely the number of points (tops or bottoms) that the trendline goes through and the length of time the trendline has persisted without being penetrated.

Figure 6–3
Down Trendline

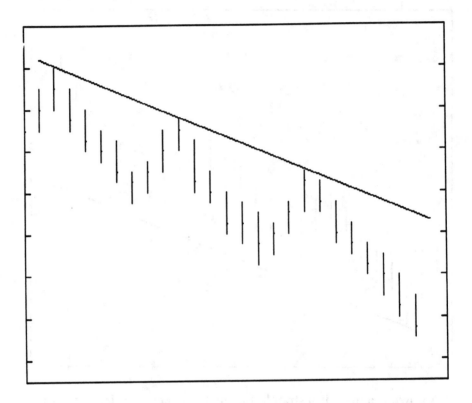

Many technicians argue that although it only takes two points (tops or bottoms) to draw a trendline, connection to a third point (top or bottom) is required for the trendline to be confirmed as valid. Each time prices move back to the trendline and then renew their advance (in the case of an up trendline) or decline (in the case of a down trendline) the significance of the trendline is enhanced.

The length of the trendline indicates the period of time that prices have remained above or below the trendline. Obviously, the longer that period is, the greater the significance of the trendline. For example, a trendline that has not been penetrated for 10 months is more significant than one that has held for 10 weeks or 10 days.

In addition to the number of points that a trendline goes through and the length of time the trendline has persisted, some technicians feel the angle of the trendline adds to the significance of a trendline. In general, the closer to horizontal the trendline is, the greater the significance of any penetration through it. Very steep trendlines can easily be broken by brief sideways consolidation moves; trendlines that are less steep are not subject to many short-term price movements (that are often inconsistent with the current trend).

Validity of Trendline Penetration

Once a trendline has been established, a change in the direction of the trend is signaled by prices breaking through the trendline. In the case of an up trend-line, this occurs as illustrated in Figure 6–4. Figure 6–5 shows the penetration of a down trendline.

Two criteria are used to determine the validity of a trendline penetration. The first criterion is the extent of penetration — how far prices have moved past the trendline. There is no right answer to the question: How far do prices

Figure 6–4
Penetration of Up Trendline

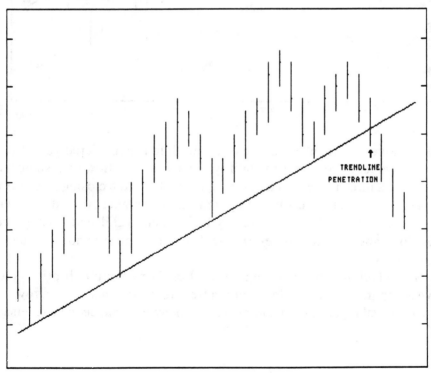

Figure 6–5
Penetration of Down Trendline

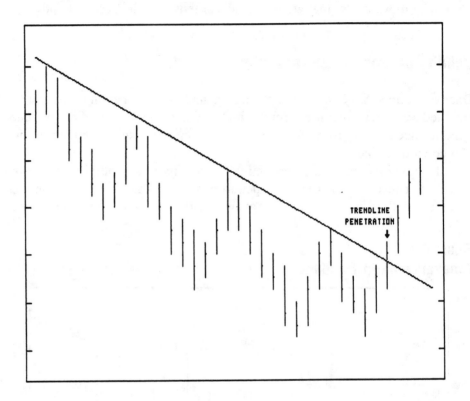

have to move before the breaking of a trendline is considered valid? It depends to a great degree on the volatility of the security. However, some technicians use a three percent rule in regard to stocks. If the closing price for the day is three percent lower (for an up trendline) or higher (for a down trendline) then the penetration is viewed as decisive and valid. The three percent move does not have to happen in one day, although it is not unusual for prices to do so.

Some technicians also use a time filter. For example, if prices close above an up trendline or below a down trendline for two days in a row, it is viewed as a valid penetration and prices are likely to continue their reversal.

TECHNICAL ANALYSIS TIP — On occasion, prices will break through an up or down trendline on an intraday basis, but then close above (in the case of an up trendline) or below (in the case of a down trendline). Is this a trendline penetration? No, most technicians look at the closing price only for trendline penetrations. However, some would redraw the trendline so that it goes through the bottom of the intraday low (for an up trendline) or the top of the intraday high (for a down trendline).

The second criterion relates to the volume. The validity of a trendline penetration is enhanced if it is accompanied by expanding volume (especially when down trendlines are broken). However, it is not essential for volume to increase for there to be a valid penetration. In other words, the extent of penetration is more important than its volume characteristics.

TECHNICAL ANALYSIS TIP — How far will prices move from a trendline once a valid penetration occurs? Typically, prices will move at least as far as the maximum distance they were on the opposite side of the trendline. For example, if the price of a stock reached $100 per share before declining and breaking through an up trendline at $80 per share, you can expect prices to fall to at least $60 per share as illustrated in Figure 6–6.

Trendline Role Reversal

Once a trendline is decisively penetrated, it normally changes its role from one of support to one of resistance for an up trendline (see Figure 6–7) or resistance to support for a down trendline (see Figure 6–8). More about support and resistance is presented in Lesson 7.

Note in both Figures 6–7 and 6–8 that prices first moved away from the trendline, then back to it, then away again. This is called a *pull-back* and is not uncommon. Pull-backs offer investors great entry points for buying or selling short.

Trend Channels

In many instances, prices repeatedly move about the same distance away from a trendline before returning to the trendline. In these cases, a straight line can be drawn connecting the peaks of rallies in an uptrend or the bottoms

Figure 6–6
Move from Trendline after Penetration

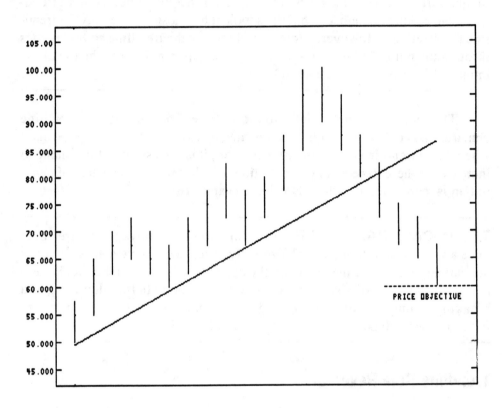

of declines in a downtrend. That line is often parallel to the trendline and is called a *return* or *channel line*. Together the channel line and trendline create a trend channel, a range within which prices are moving.

Figures 6–9 and 6–10 illustrate trend channels in an uptrend and downtrend, respectively.

Well defined trend channels appear most frequently in charts of actively traded securities. Thinly traded securities offer little opportunity for trend channels to develop.

Trend channels can be used in many fashions. Novice technicians often use trend channels to determine good profit-taking levels. For example, in an uptrend, they will sell a stock when it reaches the upper level of its trend channel.

More experienced technicians watch price movements within the two boundary lines of the trend channel looking for a warning signal that the trend

Figure 6–7
Role Reversal from Support to Resistance

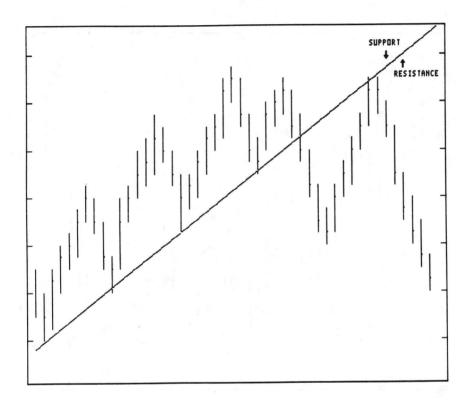

direction is changing. If, in an upward trend channel, prices rally up from the trendline but fail to reach the upper channel line, it signals a deterioration of the trend and probability that the lower line will be broken. Frequently, the distance from the top of the failed rally to the channel line equals the distance by which the next move down penetrates the trendline.

Similarly, in a downward trend channel, if prices drop from the trendline but fail to reach the bottom channel line, it signals a deterioration of the trend and probability that the upper line will be broken. Likewise, the distance from the bottom of the failed attempt to reach the channel line to the channel line often is equal to the distance by which the next rally penetrates the trendline.

Trend channels can be used in another way. If prices break through the upper line in an upward trend channel, an acceleration of the existing uptrend is signaled. At this point, some investors will buy additional positions.

Figure 6–8
Role Reversal from Resistance to Support

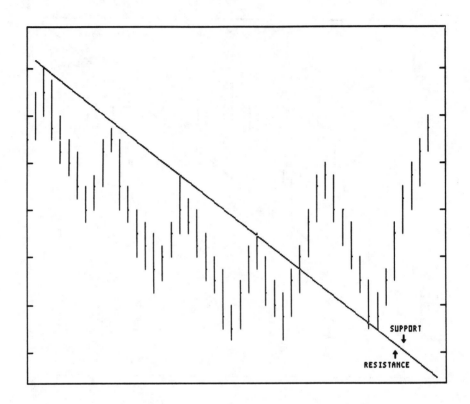

On the other hand, if prices move through the bottom line of a downward trend channel, the existing downtrend appears to be picking up pace. Short positions may be increased at this point.

The Fan Principle

One final method that uses trendlines warrants discussion. It is called the *fan principle* because it reflects the drawing of three trendlines in a fan-like appearance.

Let's examine an upward trending fan first. As illustrated in Figure 6–11, an initial trendline is drawn connecting the low prices in a normal fashion. The trendline is broken, and prices move to a lower point from which they rally back to the bottom of the trendline (which now acts as resistance instead of support). A second trendline is drawn from the low beginning of the first trendline and low of the penetration through the first trendline. Prices once again decline and break through the second trendline creating a new low. They then rally up to the bottom of the second trendline. The third and final trendline is drawn from the low beginning the first trendline and the low just created. When prices subsequently fall and break through the third trendline a reversal in prices is signaled.

A downward trending fan is illustrated in Figure 6–12. Similar to an upward trending fan, the breaking of the third trendline is what signals a reversal in prices.

Figure 6–9
Up Trend Channel

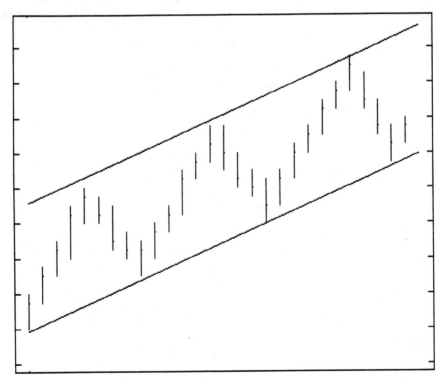

Figure 6–10
Down Trend Channel

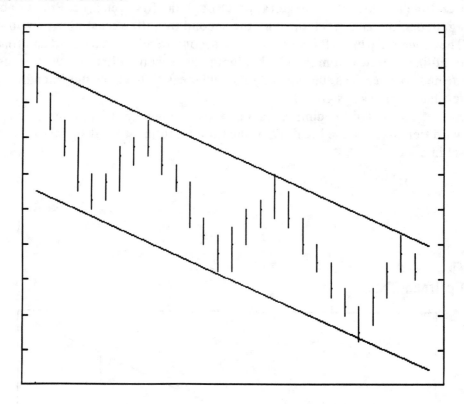

Figure 6–11
The Fan Principle—Up

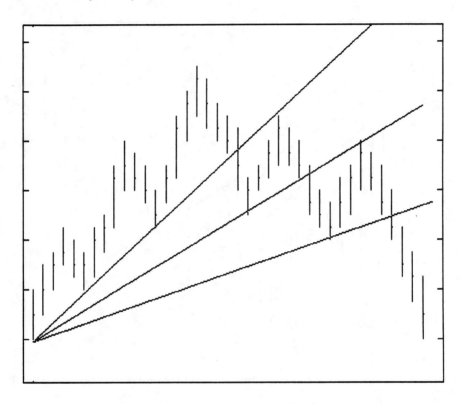

Figure 6–12
The Fan Principle—Down

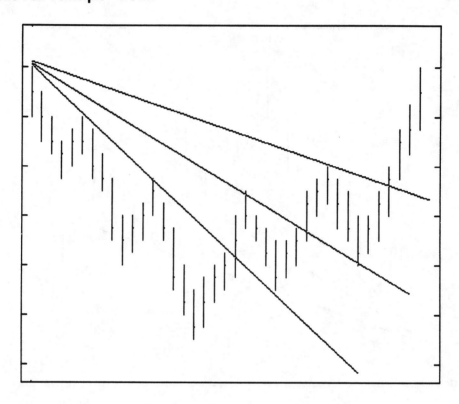

True or False Quiz

Circle T if the statement is true or F if the statement is false.

T   F   1. The trendline is one of the basic tools technicians use to identify trends and trend reversals.

T   F   2. An up trendline connects a series of rally tops.

T   F   3. Trends can be up, down, or sideways.

T   F   4. The more points that a trendline goes through, the greater the significance of a trendline.

T   F   5. A trendline that has not been penetrated for 10 months is of equal technical significance to a trendline that has not been broken for 10 weeks.

T   F   6. Once an uptrend is penetrated, it normally changes its role from one of support to one of resistance.

T   F   7. Prices seldom move about the same distance away from a trendline before returning back to the trendline.

T   F   8. Trend channels appear frequently in charts of actively traded stocks.

T   F   9. Using the fan principle, a reversal in prices is signaled when prices break through the second of three trendlines.

Answers

1. *True.*

2. *False.* An up trendline connects a series of reaction lows. See Figure 6–2.

3. *True.*

4. *True.*

5. *False.* The longer the period is that prices do not penetrate a trendline, the greater the technical significance.

6. *True.*

7. *False.* In many instances, prices repeatedly move about the same distance away from a trendline before returning back to the trendline. As a result, trend channels can be drawn as illustrated in Figure 6–9.

8. *True.*

9. *False.* Breaking of the third trendline signals a reversal in prices.

Support and Resistance

In Lesson 6, support and resistance were referred to briefly. In this lesson, the concepts of support and resistance will be more fully explained. In addition, two sophisticated applications of support and resistance, namely percentage retracements and speed resistance lines, will be examined.

Support and Resistance Defined

In the Wall Street environment, the terms *support* and *resistance* are almost synonymous with demand and supply, respectively. Support is a price level at which there is adequate demand for a security to stop its downward price movement and, normally, turn prices upward. (See Figure 7–1.) Support occurs at reaction lows.

Resistance is a price level at which there is a significant supply of a stock causing prices to halt an upward move and, typically, turn prices down. (See Figure 7–2.) Resistance occurs at reaction highs.

In an uptrend, both support and resistance levels rise as illustrated in Figure 7–3. Typically, support levels hold while resistance offers temporary halts to upward movements in prices. Resistance levels are repeatedly broken until the uptrend is reversed.

In a downtrend, both support and resistance levels move lower as illustrated in Figure 7–4. Typically, resistance levels hold while support levels temporarily stop down price movements. Support levels are repeatedly broken until the downtrend is reversed.

Figure 7–1
Support

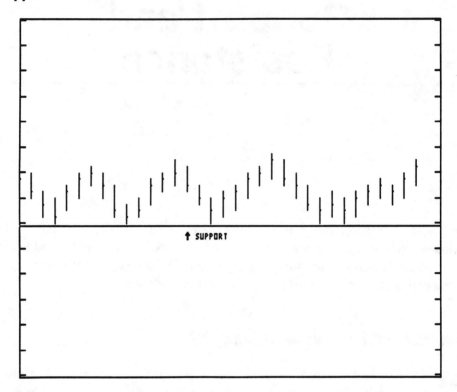

↑ SUPPORT

TECHNICAL ANALYSIS TIP — Beware of round numbers! Technicians have discovered that prices often find support or resistance at round numbers, such as 10, 20, 25, 50, 75, 100, etc. Round numbers act as psychological levels that stop advances or declines. For example, the 1000 level on the Dow Jones Industrial Average offered resistance for many years before it was penetrated.

    As a rule, don't place trading orders or protective stop-loss orders at round numbers. In an uptrend, it is better to place buy orders just above round numbers and stop loss orders just below round numbers. On the other hand, if you want to sell short in a downtrend, place your sell order just below and your stop loss order just above the appropriate round number.

    Round numbers are particularly important for short-term traders.

Figure 7–2
Resistance

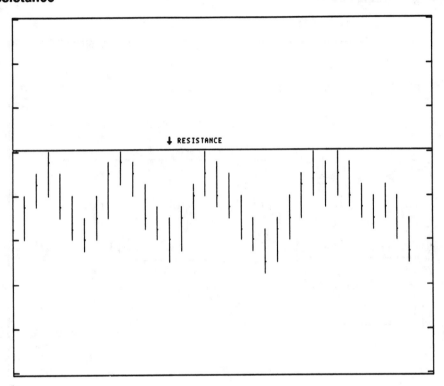

↓ RESISTANCE

Role Reversal

In an uptrend, resistance levels often become support levels after they are broken significantly as illustrated in Figure 7–5. In a downtrend, the opposite occurs as support levels frequently become resistance levels. (See Figure 7–6.)

The likelihood of role reversal, from support to resistance or resistance to support, depends on three factors. First, the greater the volume that occurrs at a support or resistance level, the more significant the level is and, thus, the more likely a candidate the level is for role reversal. Second, the longer that prices trade near the support or resistance level, the greater the chance of role reversal. For example, the probability of role reversal is enhanced if consolidation occurs near a support or resistance level for a few weeks rather than a few days. Finally, the more recently that trading occurred at the level, the

Figure 7–3
Rising Support and Resistance

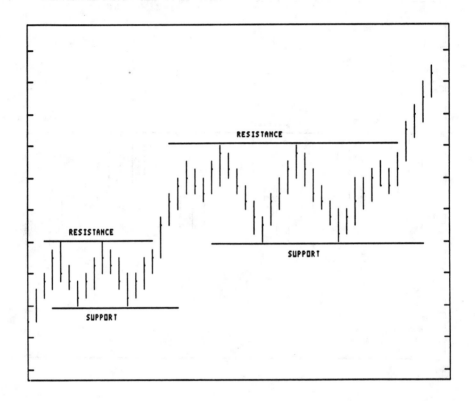

fresher it is in traders' minds, and the more likely it is that role reversal will occur.

Trend Reversals

In an uptrend, a trend reversal occurs when prices are held at a resistance level. A double top or some other reversal formation develops at that point and the trend changes direction as illustrated in Figure 7–7.

A trend reversal occurs in a downtrend when prices are unable to penetrate a support level. In this case, a bottom reversal pattern is formed, and the trend changes direction to the upside as illustrated in Figure 7–8.

Keep in mind that a trend reversal is not signaled by the first failure to break through a resistance level (in an uptrend) or a support level (in a down-

Figure 7–4
Declining Support and Resistance

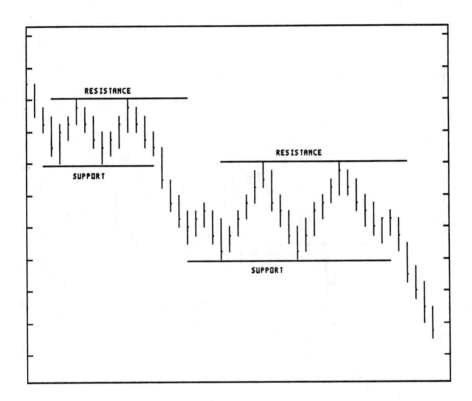

trend). A reversal pattern must fully develop before one gets the signal that the trend has changed. In other words, a trader should not rush to sell all of his or her securities or sell short just because prices have held at a resistance level. Likewise, one should not load up on securities or cover short positions just because prices initially fail to penetrate a support level. Wait for more evidence that a trend reversal is occurring.

Percentage Retracements

After prices move either up or down for a period of time, they usually move in the opposite direction, retracing a portion of the previous move. Subsequently, prices continue in the original trend direction.

Figure 7–5
Uptrend Role Reversal from Resistance to Support

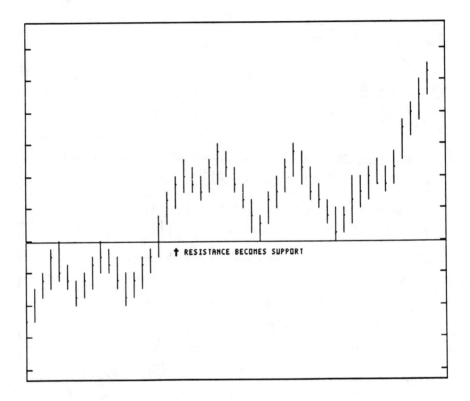

Countertrend price moves frequently move by a percentage range amount. Often prices will retrace from a minimum of one-third (or 33 percent) to a maximum of two-thirds (67 percent) of its previous move before continuing in its original trend direction. Figure 7–9 illustrates a 50 percent retracement which is very common.

Some traders view a retracement of 33 percent to 50 percent as a buying opportunity in an uptrend or a selling opportunity in a downtrend. The two-thirds level is a critical area. If prices move past the two-thirds retracement level, a trend reversal is likely.

Figure 7–6
Downtrend Role Reversal from Support to Resistance

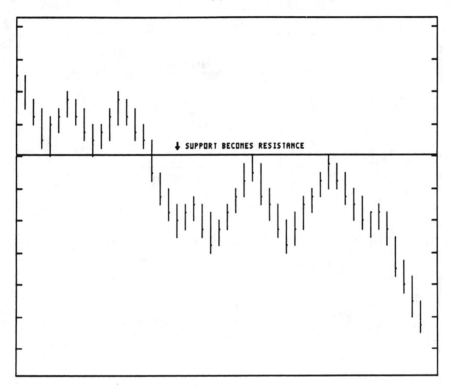

↓ SUPPORT BECOMES RESISTANCE

Speed Resistance Lines

Speed resistance lines (also known as speed lines) are based on a theory that trends are divided into thirds. Unlike percentage retracements that look at just price movements in terms of thirds, speed resistance lines look at both price and time. Speed resistance lines measure the rate at which a trend moves up or down.

In an uptrend, speed resistance lines are constructed by dividing the vertical distance from the beginning of the trend to the highest point on the chart. That distance is then divided into thirds. Two trendlines are drawn as illustrated in Figure 7–10. The first trendline is drawn from the beginning of the trend to one-third of the way up the vertical distance. The second trendline is

Figure 7–7
Trend Reversal at Top

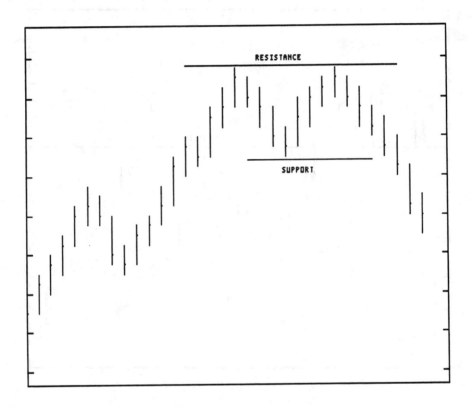

drawn from the beginning of the trend to two-thirds of the way up the vertical distance.

Figure 7–11 illustrates the construction of speed resistance lines in a downtrend. The principles are similar to those used in construction of speed resistance lines in an uptrend.

How do you use speed resistance lines? It is simple.

If, in an uptrend, prices have made a new peak and are retracing (or correcting) some of the upward movement, they will frequently stop at the two-thirds speed resistance line. If prices do not stop at the two-thirds line, they will probably move to the one-third speed resistance line. If they are not held at the one-third line, a trend reversal is signaled.

In a downtrend, breaking the two-thirds speed resistance line suggests the likelihood of a rally to the one-third line. If that is penetrated, a trend reversal is probable.

Figure 7–8
Trend Reversal at Bottom

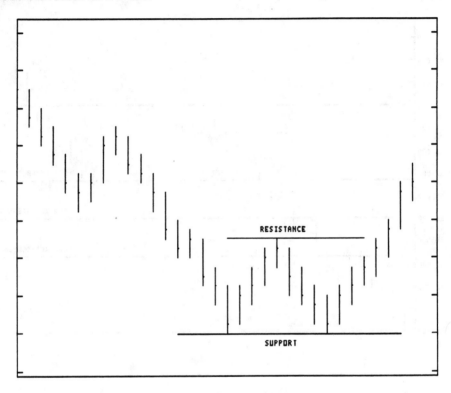

Figure 7–9
Example of Percentage Retracement

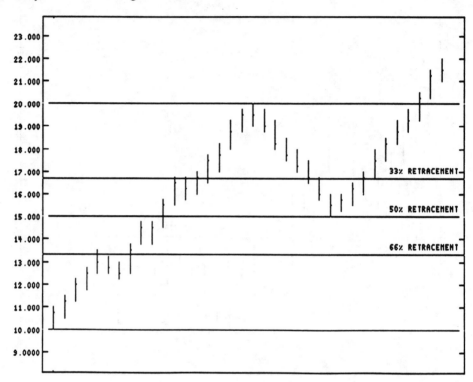

Figure 7–10
Speed Resistance Lines in an Uptrend

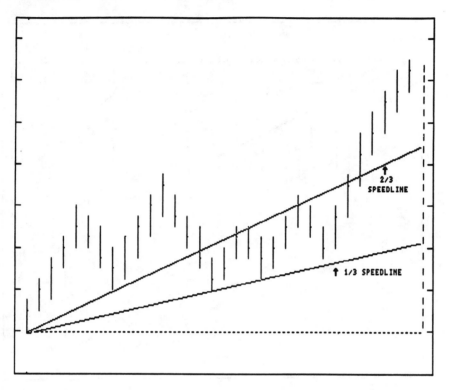

Figure 7–11
Speed Resistance Lines in a Downtrend

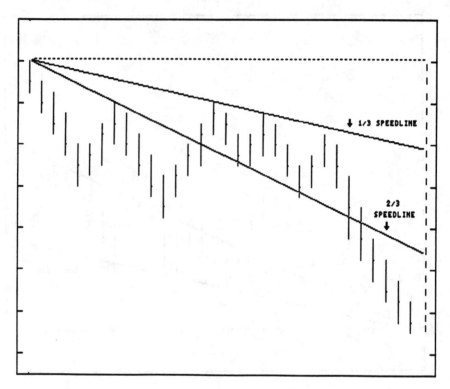

True or False Quiz

Circle T if the statement is true or F if the statement is false.

T   F   1. Support occurs at reaction lows, while resistance occurs at reaction highs.

T   F   2. In a downtrend, support levels are repeatedly broken until a reversal in prices occurs.

T   F   3. Prices seldom find support or resistance at round numbers.

T   F   4. Support levels never become resistance levels.

T   F   5. In an uptrend, a trend reversal occurs when prices are held at a resistance level.

T   F   6. Percentage retracements examine countertrend price moves in terms of thirds.

T   F   7. If prices break the two-thirds speed resistance line, the probability is that they will continue to the one-third speed resistance line.

Answers

1. *True.*

2. *True.*

3. *False.* Prices often find support or resistance at round numbers.

4. *False.* In a downtrend support levels frequently become resistance levels. See Figure 7–6.

5. *True.* See Figure 7–7.

6. *True.*

7. *True.*

LESSON 8

Using Moving Averages

One of the most widely used tools in the technician's toolbox is the *moving average*. Various types of moving averages are used to smooth price fluctuations and get a clearer picture of a security's price trend.

This lesson will show the advantages and disadvantages of simple, weighted, and exponential moving averages. It will teach how to use one moving average or two or more in combination to signal the trend of prices. In addition, the envelope (also known as a *trading band*), a moving average filter, will be discussed.

Before discussing the types of moving averages, it is important to understand exactly what a moving average is. An average is the sum of whatever you are examining (for example, the closing prices of a stock) for a number of instances (for example, 10 days) divided by the number of instances (10 days). The moving part of moving average means that one recalculates the average for each additional instance (day).

Simple Moving Average

The simple moving average is used by many technicians because it is the easiest type of moving average to calculate, and it is fairly effective. It is equivalent to the moving arithmetic mean.

The simple moving average is calculated by adding the prices (typically closing prices) for a number of periods (hours, days, weeks, etc.) and dividing by the number of periods. Let's look at an example. Table 8–1 shows sample closing price data for 20 days, as well as how to calculate a five-day simple moving average. You simply add up the last five days' closing prices and divide by five.

Table 8-1
Calculating a Five-Day Simple Moving Average

Date	Closing price	Five-day total (A)	Five-day simple moving average (A)/5
March 22	45.375		
March 23	45.500		
March 24	45.000		
March 25	43.625		
March 28	43.375	222.875	44.575
March 29	43.125	220.625	44.125
March 30	43.125	218.250	43.650
March 31	44.250	217.500	43.500
April 4	43.500	217.375	43.475
April 5	44.375	218.375	43.675
April 6	45.875	221.125	44.225
April 7	46.750	224.750	44.950
April 8	47.625	228.125	45.625
April 11	48.000	232.625	46.525
April 12	49.125	237.375	47.475
April 13	48.750	240.250	48.050
April 14	46.125	239.625	47.925
April 15	46.750	238.750	47.750
April 18	46.625	237.375	47.475
April 19	46.000	234.250	46.850

Figure 8-1 shows the five-day simple moving average plotted on a bar chart. Note that there is no simple moving average charted for the first four days, since there is not enough data to make the calculation until the fifth day.

Longer time periods are typically used for simple moving averages. For example, the commonly used 200-day simple moving average of the New York Stock Exchange Composite Index closing prices is plotted in Figure 8-2. As a rule of thumb, as long as the Index is above its 200-day simple moving average, the outlook is bullish. On the other hand, when it falls below its 200-day simple moving average, it is a bearish sign.

A major criticism of the simple moving average is that it gives equal weight to each period's price rather than weighting recent periods' action heavier than older periods' price action. Both weighted and exponential moving averages answer that criticism.

Figure 8–1
Five-Day Simple Moving Average of Example Data

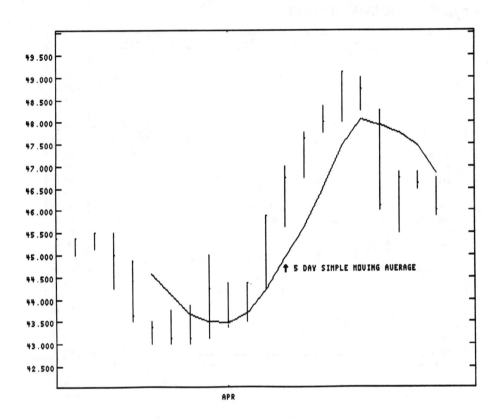

APR

TECHNICAL ANALYSIS TIP — Recalculating simple moving averages on a daily (or other period) basis is easy. Suppose you are calculating a 50-day simple moving average. You don't have to add up the prices for 50 days every day. Here's how you do it and save a lot of time.

The first day you add up the 50 prices. Write down your total before you divide by 50 to calculate the average. The second day take that total, add the new day's price, and subtract the oldest day's price (50 days ago). Then divide by 50.

Repeat the process on a daily basis.

Figure 8–2
200-Day Simple Moving Average of the New York Stock Exchange
Composite Index Closing Prices

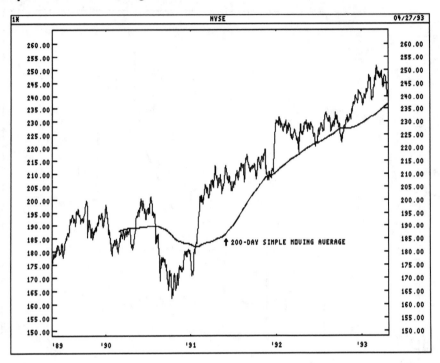

Weighted Moving Average

The weighted moving average gives each period's price a "weight" based on its age. The oldest period's price is given a weight of 1. The next to the oldest period's price is given a weight of 2. The next period's price is given a weight of 3. The price for the period after that is given a weight of 4. The weight increases by 1 until the final period (the current period) is assigned a weight.

Each period's price is multiplied by the given weight. The products of the calculation are summed and divided by the total of the weights.

Let's look at an example. Table 8–2 illustrates the calculation of a weighted moving average for a five-day period. The first day's price, which is the oldest day, is multiplied by the weight of 1. The second day's price is multiplied by 2. The third, fourth, and fifth days' prices are multiplied by 3,

Table 8–2
Calculating a Five-Day Weighted Moving Average

Date	Closing price	Closing price four days ago times 1 (A)	Closing price three days ago times 2 (B)	Closing price two days ago times 3 (C)	Closing price one day ago times 4 (D)	Today's closing price times 5 (E)	Five-day total of closing prices times weightings (A+B+C+D+E) = (F)	Five-day weighted moving average (F) / 15
03/22	45.375							
03/23	45.500							
03/24	45.000							
03/25	43.625							
03/28	43.375	45.375	91.000	135.000	174.500	216.875	662.750	44.183
03/29	43.125	45.500	90.000	130.875	173.500	215.625	655.500	43.700
03/30	43.125	45.000	87.250	130.125	172.500	215.625	650.500	43.367
03/31	44.250	43.625	86.750	129.375	172.500	221.250	653.500	43.567
04/04	43.500	43.375	86.250	129.375	177.000	217.500	653.500	43.567
04/05	44.375	43.125	86.250	132.750	174.000	221.875	658.000	43.867
04/06	45.875	43.125	88.500	130.500	177.500	229.375	669.000	44.600
04/07	46.750	44.250	87.000	133.125	183.500	233.750	681.625	45.442
04/08	47.625	43.500	88.750	137.625	187.000	238.125	695.000	46.333
04/11	48.000	44.375	91.750	140.250	190.500	240.000	706.875	47.125
04/12	49.125	45.875	93.500	142.875	192.000	245.625	719.875	47.992
04/13	48.750	46.750	95.250	144.000	196.500	243.750	726.250	48.417
04/14	46.125	47.625	96.000	147.375	195.000	230.625	716.625	47.775
04/15	46.750	48.000	98.250	146.250	184.500	233.750	710.750	47.383
04/18	46.625	49.125	97.500	138.375	187.000	233.125	705.125	47.008
04/19	46.000	48.750	92.250	140.250	186.500	230.000	697.750	46.517

Figure 8–3
Five-Day Weighted Moving Average of Example Data

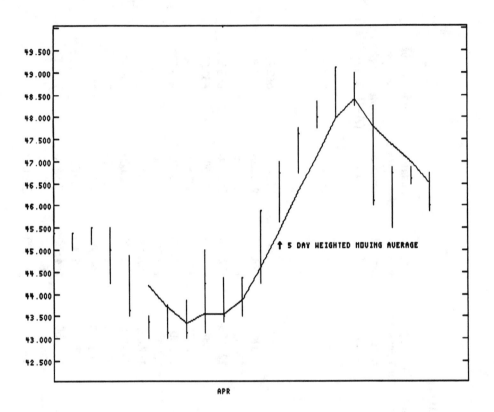

4, and 5, respectively. The products of the five calculations are summed and the total is divided by the total of the weights (1 + 2 + 3 + 4 + 5 = 15). Figure 8–3 shows graphically the five-day exponential moving average. Figure 8–4 illustrates a 200-day exponential moving average of the New York Stock Exchange Composite Index closing prices.

Exponential Moving Average

One criticism of both the simple and weighted moving average is that they include data for only the number of periods the moving average covers. For example, a five-day simple or weighted moving average only uses five days' worth of data. Data prior to those five days are not included in the calculation of the moving average.

Figure 8–4
200-Day Weighted Moving Average of the New York Stock Exchange Composite Index Closing Prices

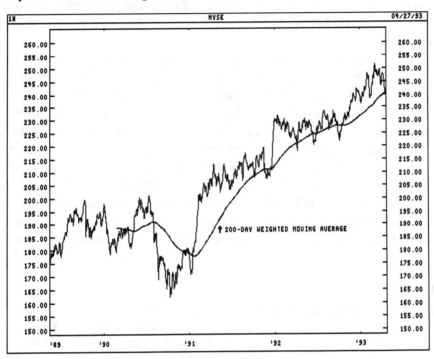

TECHNICAL ANALYSIS TIP — How many periods should you use when calculating a moving average? There is no magic answer. The "best" number of periods to use varies significantly from security to security and depends on your investment time horizon (short-, intermediate-, or long-term). You will have to test a number of different periods for each security you are examining to determine an optimal number of periods to use in calculating a moving average.

As a rule of thumb, the shorter the average, the greater the number of trend signals (including false ones).

Many technicians believe that the prior data is an important reflection of prices and should be included (on a weighted basis with older data given less weight) in a moving average calculation. These technicians frequently use an exponential moving average to accomplish that task.

An exponential moving average gives more weight to recent prices and ever-decreasing weight to older data. Unlike simple and weighted moving averages, the older data never goes away in the calculation of exponential moving averages.

The formula for calculating exponential moving averages is somewhat complex and is best done with the aid of a computer. However, let's look at a basic example in order to show, in principle, how it is calculated.

Table 8–3 illustrates the calculation of a five-day exponential moving average of closing prices. Before calculating the exponential moving average on a daily basis, you must have a beginning moving average number (previous day's exponential moving average). To start, use a five-day simple moving average for the previous day's exponential moving average. Each day you make the following calculation: The previous day's exponential moving average is subtracted from the current day's closing price. That difference is multiplied by the exponential moving average exponent (in this case, 0.4) to

Table 8–3
Calculating a Five-Day Exponential Moving Average

Date	Closing price (A)	Previous day's EMA (B)	Closing price minus previous day's EMA (A) - (B) = (C)	Difference times smoothing constant (C) times 0.4=(D)	Five-day EMA previous day's EMA + (D)
March 22	45.375				
March 23	45.500				
March 24	45.000				
March 25	43.625				
March 28	43.375	44.575*	-1.200	-0.480	44.095
March 29	43.125	44.095	-0.970	-0.388	43.707
March 30	43.125	43.707	-0.582	-0.233	43.474
March 31	44.250	43.474	0.776	0.310	43.785
April 4	43.500	43.785	-0.285	-0.114	43.671
April 5	44.375	43.671	0.704	0.282	43.952
April 6	45.875	43.952	1.923	0.769	44.721
April 7	46.750	44.721	2.029	0.811	45.533
April 8	47.625	45.533	2.092	0.837	46.370
April 11	48.000	46.370	1.630	0.652	47.022
April 12	49.125	47.022	2.103	0.841	47.863
April 13	48.750	47.863	0.887	0.355	48.218
April 14	46.125	48.218	-2.093	-0.837	47.381
April 15	46.750	47.381	-0.631	-0.252	47.128
April 18	46.625	47.128	-0.503	-0.201	46.927
April 19	46.000	46.927	-0.927	-0.371	46.556

*Five-day simple moving average.

arrive at a number that is added (or subtracted, if negative) to the previous day's exponential moving average resulting in the current day's exponential moving average.

The exponent for a given time period is calculated by dividing 2 by the number of time periods in the exponential moving average. Thus, for five periods, the exponential equals 2 divided by 5 or 0.4. Some other examples of exponents follow:

Number of Periods	Exponent
10	0.2
20	0.1
50	0.04
200	0.01

Figure 8–5 shows graphically a five-day exponential moving average of the data presented in Table 8–3.

Figure 8–5
Five-Day Exponential Moving Average of Example Data

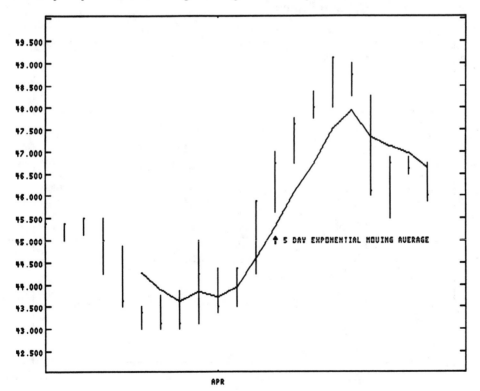

Figure 8–6 illustrates a 200-day exponential moving average of the New York Stock Exchange Composite Index closing prices.

TECHNICAL ANALYSIS TIP — Which type of moving average — simple, weighted, or exponential — is best? There is no correct answer. In many cases, a simple moving average will work just as well as the much more difficult to calculate exponential moving average. However, as a rule, the exponential moving average is more sensitive to changes in price than the simple moving average, but less than the weighted moving average. Once again, you must experiment to see which type of moving average (as well as which number of periods of time) will work best with the investment opportunity you are analyzing.

Figure 8–6
200-Day Exponential Moving Average of the New York Stock Exchange Composite Index Closing Prices

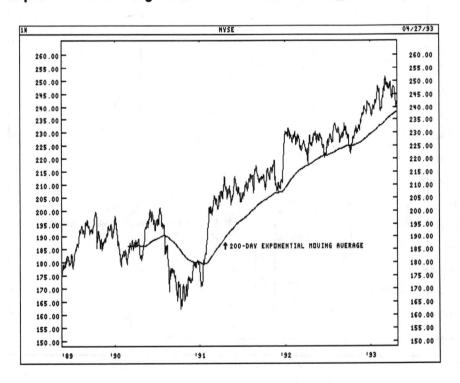

Multiple Moving Averages

Moving averages of differing lengths are often used together in trend determination. The objective of using more than one moving average is to reduce whipsaw trades.

When two moving averages are used, a buy signal is given when the shorter-term moving average crosses above the longer-term moving average. A sell signal occurs when the opposite happens: the longer-term moving average crosses above the shorter-term moving average. Figure 8–7 shows 5- and 20-day simple moving averages for PepsiCo and the signals they generate in combination. Note that the shorter five-day simple moving average is much more sensitive to trend changes than the longer 20-day simple moving average. Three moving averages can also be used in a triple crossover method. A popular combination employs 4-, 9-, and 18-day moving averages. It is princi-

Figure 8–7
Comparison of 5- and 20-Day Simple Moving Averages for PepsiCo

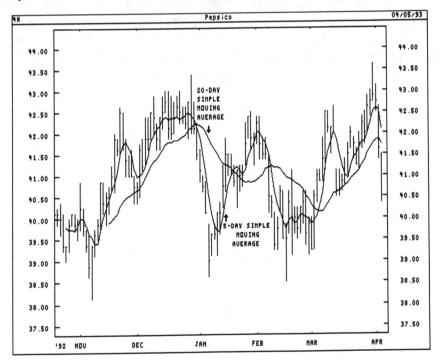

pally used with commodities. A buy signal is generated when both the four (acts as a warning) and nine (acts as a confirmation) day moving averages cross above the 18-day moving average. Sell signals are produced by the crossing of the four- and nine-day moving averages below the 18-day moving average.

Envelopes (Trading Bands)

Envelopes (also known as trading bands) create a filter around a moving average line. Two lines, one above and one below, are drawn parallel to the moving average. The distance between the moving average and the upper and lower envelope lines is a certain percentage. That percentage amount depends on the particular trading technique one is employing.

One common use of envelopes is to signal when prices are particularly strong or weak. For example, Figure 8–8 shows Standard & Poor's 500 Index daily data with a 21-day simple moving average line and envelope lines at 3.5 percent above and below the moving average line. The vast majority of the time, prices will trade within plus or minus 3.5 percent of the moving average line. If prices break above the upper envelope line, prices are accelerating faster than normal, implying great market strength and a continued move upward in prices. If, on the other hand, prices fall below the lower envelope line, great market weakness is suggested, as well as a further decline in prices.

Figure 8–8
Three and a Half Percent Envelope Around a 21-Day Simple Moving
Average of the Standard & Poor's 500 Index

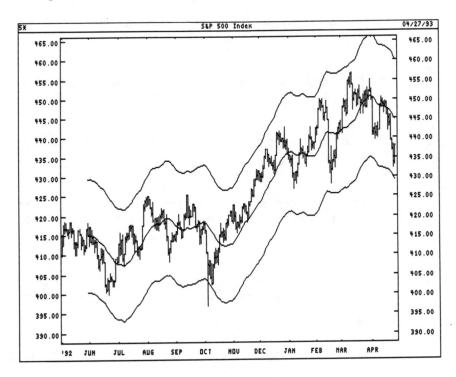

True or False Quiz

Circle T if the statement is true or F if the statement is false.

T   F   1. The weighted moving average is the easiest type of moving average to calculate.

T   F   2. The simple moving average gives equal weight to each period's price.

T   F   3. When prices are above a moving average line, it is generally viewed as bullish.

T   F   4. When calculating a weighted moving average, older periods' prices are given more weight than more current periods' prices.

T   F   5. A five-day weighted moving average will normally generate more signals than a 50-day weighted moving average.

T   F   6. Unlike simple and weighted moving averages, older data never goes away in the calculation of exponential moving averages.

T   F   7. Normally, the simple moving average is more sensitive to price changes than the exponential moving average.

T   F   8. When two moving averages are used, a buy signal is given when the shorter-term moving average crosses above the longer-term moving average.

T   F   9. When using a combination of four-, nine-, and 18-day moving averages, a buy signal is produced by a crossing of both the four- and the nine-day moving averages below the 18-day moving average.

T   F   10. Envelopes are two lines, one above and one below, drawn parallel to the moving average.

Answers

1. *False.* The simple moving average is the easiest type of moving average to calculate.

2. *True.*

3. *True.*

4. *False.* Older periods' prices are given less weight than more current periods' prices in the calculation of a weighted moving average.

5. *True.*

6. *True.*

7. *False.* Since it gives more weight to the latest prices, the exponential moving average is normally more sensitive to price changes than the simple moving average.

8. *True.*

9. *False.* A buy signal is generated when both the four- and nine-day moving averages cross above the 18-day moving average. A sell signal is produced by a crossing of both the four- and nine-day moving averages below the 18-day moving average.

10. *True.*

Relative Strength Analysis

Relative strength analysis is an easy concept to understand. It simply compares the performance of one item (such as a stock) with another item (such as an industry group). The objective is to determine if the first item's price is advancing or declining faster than the second item's price. In other words, is the first item outperforming or underperforming the second item on a relative basis. Relative strength analysis is normally used to compare an industry group's performance to the overall market or a particular stock's performance to its industry group. However, it can also be used to compare virtually any two items as long as they have prices (such as two stocks, two commodities, two industry groups, etc.).

Industry Group versus a Market Index

Technicians compare industry groups to the market as a whole using relative strength analysis to determine which industry groups are outperforming or underperforming the overall market. A ranking of the various industry groups can be made according to their relative strength. Those industry groups with the highest rankings are candidates for buying; whereas those with low rankings represent potential selling or short sales.

Figure 9–1 compares the telecommunications industry group to the Standard & Poor's 500 Index. Note that the industry's relative strength rose over the last several months. Therefore, it represents an industry group that is out-performing the market (as of the time this relative strength analysis was performed).

Figure 9–1
Telecommunications Industry Group (Top)
and Relative Strength of the Telecommunications Industry Group
versus the Standard & Poor's 500 Index (Bottom)

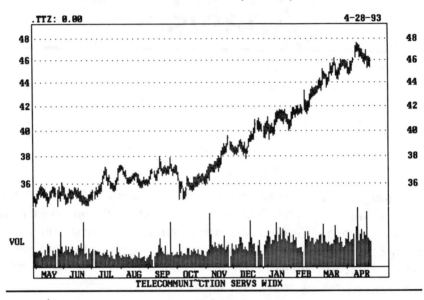

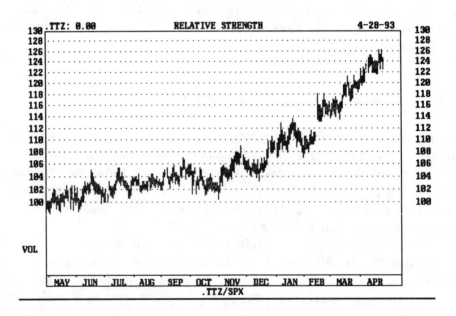

Source: By permission of Telescan, Inc.

Figure 9–2 demonstrates an industry group (medical-drugs) with declining relative strength when compared to the Standard & Poor's 500 Index. Thus, it is underperforming the market as a whole (as of the time this relative strength analysis was performed).

TECHNICAL ANALYSIS TIP — Use a top down approach when performing relative strength analysis. First, determine which industry groups are outperforming the overall market. Then, determine which stocks in the highest ranking industry group are outperforming the industry group. Finally, use the various entry technical analysis tools (such as chart patterns, moving averages, etc.) to find a good time to buy one or more of the stocks that have demonstrated strength by outperforming others.

Individual Stock versus an Industry Group

In a fashion similar to comparing an industry group to the overall market, a technician can use relative strength analysis to compare an individual stock's price performance to that of the industry to which it belongs.

Let's look at an example. Figure 9–3 compares the performance of Sprint to the telecommunications industry group. The rising relative strength of the stock when compared to the industry as a whole suggests the stock's performance has been relatively strong. It should be considered for purchase in an uptrend.

On the other hand, stocks with low relative strengths when compared to industry groups or the overall stock market may represent good short selling opportunities.

Keep in mind the old Wall Street saying "the trend is your friend." Don't buy stocks just because their relative strength is high or sell stocks solely on the basis of low relative strengths. Look at the overall trend of the market. In an uptrend, buy high relative strength stocks. In a downtrend, sell or sell short low relative strength stocks.

TECHNICAL ANALYSIS TIP — Relative strength numbers are available from numerous investment services. However, a very inexpensive source of relative strength numbers is *Investor's Business Daily*. Each day it publishes the latest relative strength numbers for thousands of individual stocks and about 200 industry groups.

Figure 9–2
**Medical-Drugs Industry Group (Top) and Relative Strength of the
Medical-Drugs Industry Group versus the Standard & Poor's 500 Index
(Bottom)**

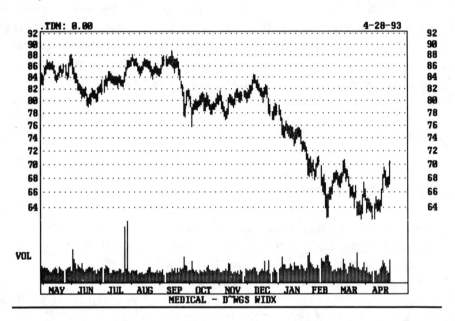

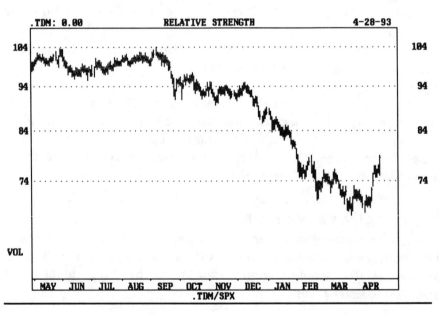

Source: By permission of Telescan, Inc.

Figure 9–3
Sprint (Top) and Relative Strength of Sprint
versus the Telecommunications Industry Group (Bottom)

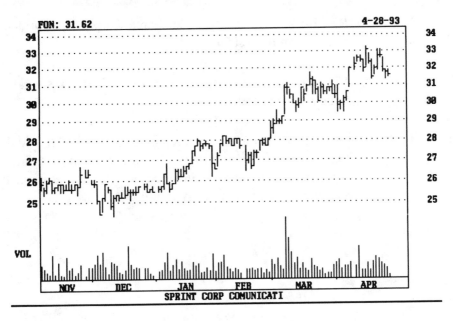

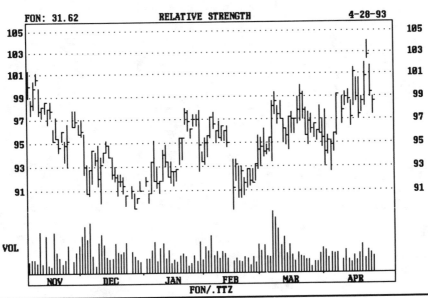

Source: By permission of Telescan, Inc.

True or False Quiz

Circle T if the statement is true or F if the statement is false.

T   F   1. Relative strength analysis compares the price performance of one item to another.

T   F   2. If the relative strength of a stock is high, it should be bought immediately.

T   F   3. When market prices are moving up, a stock with a higher than average relative strength when compared to its industry group is moving up in price at a faster rate than the average stock in its industry group.

Answers

1. *True.*

2. *False.* Even if the relative strength of a stock is high, one should perform further analysis to determine if the market is in an uptrend and use the various technical analysis tools to find a good entry time to buy the stock. Don't forget, if the overall market is going down, the probability is very high that the stock being examined is going down too (regardless of how high its relative strength is).

3. *True.*

Volume and Open Interest

The majority of what was presented in the lessons thus far has related to two dimensions of market analysis, namely time and price. Most technicians examine a third dimension, which is *volume*. In addition, commodity traders analyze open interest numbers for supply and demand considerations.

Basic Rules of Volume

Historically, volume has related to market prices as follows:

Price	Volume	Implication
Rising	Up	Bullish
Rising	Down	Bearish
Declining	Up	Bearish
Declining	Down	Bullish

Volume is viewed as a measure of market strength or weakness. If volume is increasing while prices are moving either up or down, it is likely that prices will continue their current price trend. On the other hand, a decline in volume is considered to signal that steam is running out in the direction of the current trend and consolidation or a reversal could be forthcoming.

TECHNICAL ANALYSIS TIP — The advent of program trading, dividend recapture programs, and other new market instruments has, at least temporarily, diminished the value of volume indicators. That doesn't mean you shouldn't examine them. Just view them with a grain of salt — they are not as reliable as they once were.

Blowoffs and Selling Climaxes

Dramatic market action that is common at market tops and bottoms is known as *blowoffs* and *selling climaxes*.

Blowoffs occur at market tops. They usually occur after prices have moved higher over an extended period of time. At the end of the up move, prices rally sharply accompanied by a large increase in volume. Typically, all of those that were going to buy at this level have done so. Profit taking occurs and prices reverse, often suddenly, to the downside.

Selling climaxes are simply the opposite of blowoffs. They occur at market bottoms after prices have been declining for an extended period of time. One final wave of selling drives prices sharply lower on significantly increased volume. Bargain hunters then jump in buying, reversing the trend, and sending prices higher.

On-Balance Volume

On-Balance Volume is a technique of volume analysis that has been popularized by Joseph E. Granville, author of *A New Strategy of Daily Stock Market Timing for Maximum Profit* (Prentice-Hall, Englewood Cliffs, NJ, 1976).

On-Balance Volume is calculated in two steps. First, each day's total volume is deemed as being positive or negative depending on whether prices closed higher or lower for the day. If prices close higher, the total volume is positive; if prices close lower, the total volume is negative. Second, each day's positive or negative value is summed in a running cumulative total.

The actual value of On-Balance Volume is not important. Its direction relative to market price provides clues to buying and selling pressure. (See Figure 10–1 for an example.)

Figure 10–1
Example of On-Balance Volume: General Electric Price Chart (Top)
versus On-Balance Volume Chart for General Electric (Bottom)

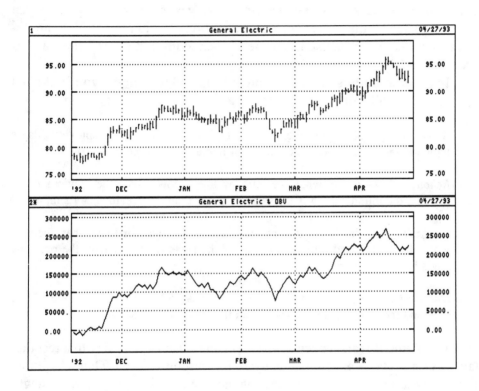

As with many cumulative indicators (such as the advance-decline line),
On-Balance Volume is interpreted as follows using divergence analysis:

Price	On-Balance Volume	Interpretation
Rising	Rising	Bullish
Rising	Declining	Bearish
Declining	Rising	Bullish
Declining	Declining	Bearish

Volume Reversal

Another method of volume analysis is the *Volume Reversal* technique, which was implemented and refined by Mark Leibovit.[*] It is based on the concept that volume precedes price and, therefore, changes in the trend of prices often can be signaled by the expansion and contraction of volume. The Volume Reversal technique can be used to project stock, commodity, or index futures prices.

In order to understand the Volume Reversal technique, you first must understand the following definitions:

Rally Day—A day when the intraday high is higher than the previous day's high and the intraday low is the same or higher than the previous day's low.

Reaction Day—A day when the intraday low is lower than the previous day's low and the intraday high is the same or lower than the previous day's high.

Inside Day—A day when the intraday high is the same or lower than the previous day's high and the intraday low is the same or higher than the previous day's low.

Outside Day—A day when the intraday high is higher than the previous day's high and the intraday low is lower than the previous day's low.

A Volume Reversal occurs when a change from a rally day to a reaction day, or vice versa, is accompanied by an increase in volume. Thus, if volume increases and the criteria for a reaction day are met, it is considered a negative Volume Reversal and time to sell. If, on the other hand, volume increases and the criteria for a rally day are met, it is considered a positive Volume Reversal and time to buy. Inside and outside days are ignored in the Volume Reversal technique.

Let's look at two examples, one illustrating a negative Volume Reversal and one showing a positive Volume Reversal.

---

[*] Volume Reversal is a registered trademark of Almarco Trading Corporation, the publisher of Mark Leibovit's *The Volume Reversal Survey*, a semimonthly market newsletter. A 32-page booklet, *Using the Volume Reversal Survey in Market Analysis*, is available for a fee from Almarco Trading Corporation, P.O. Box 1451, Sedona, AZ 86336.

Example 1
Dow Jones Industrial Average January 6-11, 1984

1984	High	Low	Close	Dow 30 Industrial Volume
Jan. 6	1293.66	1271.78	1286.75	15,403
9	1295.32	1275.85	1286.22	15,076
10	1295.44	1273.97	1278.48	12,470
11	1284.13	1267.59	1277.32	17,253

In Example 1, note that January 9 was a rally day (higher high and higher low) followed by an outside day (higher high and lower low) on January 10. On January 11, a reaction day (lower high and lower low) occurred accompanied by an increase in volume signaling a negative Volume Reversal and time to sell.

Example 2
Dow Jones Industrial Average February 22-24, 1984

1984	High	Low	Close	Dow 30 Industrial Volume
Feb. 22	1145.83	1128.66	1134.21	8,925
23	1142.38	1114.95	1134.63	9,042
24	1167.09	1137.04	1165.10	10,005

In Example 2, a positive Volume Reversal signaled that it was time to buy. February 23 was a reaction day (lower high and lower low) immediately followed on February 24 by a rally day (higher high and higher low) accompanied by greater volume.

One final point: The closing price is not used in the Volume Reversal technique. The technique assumes that the range between the low and the high of a day gives a better indication of what actually is happening than the price at the end of the day.

Open Interest

Open interest is the number of contracts that are trading for a particular commodity. The basic rules for open interest are similar to those for volume. They are as follows:

Price	Open Interest	Interpretation
Rising	Up	Bullish
Rising	Down	Bearish
Declining	Up	Bearish
Declining	Down	Bullish

Expanding open interest in an uptrend represents aggressive new buying and is bullish. On the other hand, expanding open interest in a downtrend represents aggressive new short selling and is bearish.

Declining open interest in an uptrend represents short covering, not new buying, and is bearish. However, declining open interest in a downtrend suggests the liquidation of losing long positions and is bullish.

TECHNICAL ANALYSIS TIP — At the end of an up move in prices, a leveling off or decline in open interest should serve as a warning that a reversal in the trend of prices is forthcoming.

True or False Quiz

Circle T if the statement is true or F if the statement is false.

T   F   1. If a stock's price is rising accompanied by increasing volume, it is viewed as bullish.

T   F   2. If a stock's price is declining accompanied by increasing volume, it is viewed as bullish.

T   F   3. Blowoffs occur at market bottoms when a final wave of selling drives prices sharply lower on significantly increased volume.

T   F   4. Divergence analysis is used to interpret On-Balance Volume as bullish or bearish for prices.

T   F   5. A positive Volume Reversal occurs when volume increases and the criteria for a rally day are met.

T   F   6. Expanding open interest in a downtrend represents aggressive new buying and is bullish.

Answers

1. *True.*

2. *False.* If a stock's price is declining on increasing volume, it is considered bearish.

3. *False.* Selling climaxes occur at market bottoms; blowoffs occur at market tops.

4. *True.*

5. *True.*

6. *False.* Expanding open interest in a downtrend represents aggressive new short selling and is bearish.

ADVANCED
ANALYSIS

Oscillators

Oscillators serve many purposes, but they are primarily designed to give a clearer picture of market action. They are relatively easy to construct and interpret.

One of the virtues of oscillators is that they can be used regardless of whether prices are moving up, down, or sideways. Many other technical tools have diminished value when prices are moving sideways.

This lesson will examine the three main types of oscillators and the methods used to interpret each.

Oscillator Interpretation

Oscillators are typically constructed with lower and upper boundaries, such as -1 to +1 or 0 to 100. Oscillator readings range between the lower and upper boundaries. Typically, peaks and lows in the oscillator correspond to peaks and lows in market prices.

Before describing the three main types of oscillators, let's examine three common methods of interpreting oscillators.

Crossing of the Midpoint Line　When the oscillator crosses the midpoint line, a signal is given that prices will move in the direction of the crossing. If the oscillator moves up through the midpoint line, it is bullish. On the other hand, if the oscillator declines through the midpoint line, it is considered to be a bearish sign for prices.

The midpoint line is typically zero for oscillators that range from negative to positive numbers (i.e., -1 to +1). For oscillators with lower and upper boundaries of 0 and 100, the midpoint line is 50.

TECHNICAL ANALYSIS TIP — The saying "Don't fight the trend!" is frequently heard on Wall Street. Keep in mind that you will have a greater probability of success when you follow oscillator signals from midpoint line crossovers if they are in the direction of the prevailing trend in prices.

Divergence Analysis   When market prices make a high, correct, and then make a new high, and at the same time, the oscillator makes a high, corrects, and then does not make a new high, a bearish divergence occurs. That suggests that market prices are likely to go lower.

Similarly, when market prices make a low, correct, and then make a new low, and the oscillator makes a corresponding low, corrects, and then does not reach a new low, a bullish divergence occurs. The implication of a bullish divergence is that market prices are likely to rise.

Extreme Readings   Extreme high readings suggest an overbought condition and are, therefore, viewed as bearish. Extreme low readings are interpreted as prices reaching an oversold condition that is bullish. Note that oscillators can remain at extreme readings for lengthy periods of time. Thus, it is best to recognize extreme readings as periods of market vulnerability and not as specific buy and sell signals.

Types of Oscillators

There are three main types of oscillators:

1.   Momentum oscillators.
2.   Rate of change oscillators.
3.   Moving average oscillators.

Each type will be described in detail in the following sections.

Momentum Oscillators

Momentum measures the acceleration or deceleration of prices rather than actual price levels. A *momentum oscillator* is constructed to measure that speed or rate of change.

To create a momentum oscillator, subtract the closing period's price for a certain number of period's ago from the current period's closing price. Do this each period and plot the amounts calculated. For example, a five-day momentum oscillator is the difference between the current day's closing price and the closing price five days ago. Each day this positive or negative value is plotted around the zero line as illustrated in Figure 11–1 for the Standard & Poor's 500 Index.

The following table shows how the momentum oscillator reacts based on the price gains for the current period's activity versus those for N periods ago. Note that N can be any number of periods one chooses.

Momentum Oscillator	Description
Up	Prices rose by more (or declined by less) in the current period than N periods ago.
Flat	Prices rose or declined by an equal amount in the current period than N periods ago.
Down	Prices rose by less (or declined by more) in the current period than N periods ago.

One of the benefits of the momentum oscillator is that it leads price action at market turning points. It then flattens out while the current price trend is in effect.

Rate of Change Oscillators

Rate of change oscillators are simply momentum oscillators in percentage rather than point change form. They are constructed as the ratio of the current closing price to the price a certain number of periods ago. For example, a five-day rate of change oscillator is calculated by dividing the current day's closing price by the closing price five days ago. Often the calculated rate of change value is multiplied by 100 and shown in percentage terms. In such a case, the oscillator will fluctuate above and below the 100 level.

Figure 11–2 illustrates a five-day rate of change oscillator for the Standard & Poor's 500 Index.

Moving Average Oscillators

A *moving average oscillator* is constructed by taking the difference between two moving averages of different lengths and plotting that difference. The dif-

Figure 11–1
Standard & Poor's 500 Index (Top)
versus Five-Day Momentum Oscillator (Bottom)

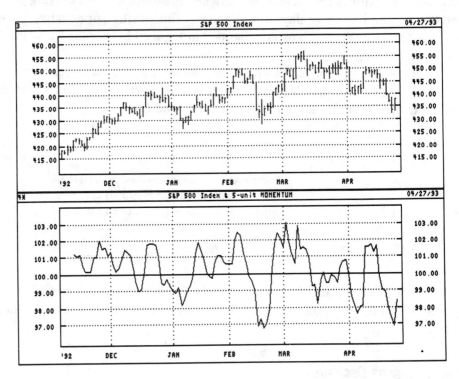

ference can be the point difference or percentage difference between the two moving averages.

The purposes of constructing a moving average oscillator are to:

1. Identify divergences.

2. Note significant deviations caused by the shorter-term moving average moving far away from the longer-term moving average.

3. To make moving average crossovers easy to see. When the oscillator crosses the zero line, the two moving averages have crossed each other.

**Figure 11–2
Standard & Poor's 500 Index (Top)
versus Five-Day Rate of Change Oscillator (Bottom)**

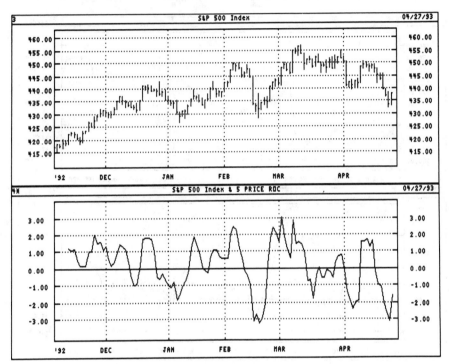

Let's look at an example. Exhibit 11–3 shows an oscillator based on 10-
and 50-day simple moving averages of the Standard & Poor's 500 Index.
Note that when the 10-day moving average is above the 50-day moving average, the oscillator is at a positive value. On the other hand, when the 10-day
moving average is below the 50-day moving average, the oscillator reading is
negative.

Figure 11–3
Standard & Poor's 500 Index (Top)
versus 10/50-Day Moving Average Oscillator (Bottom)

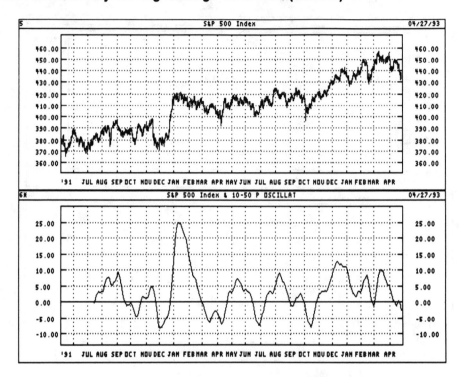

True or False Quiz

Circle T if the statement is true or F if the statement is false.

T   F   1. Oscillators are ineffective when market prices are moving in a sideways manner.

T   F   2. If a momentum oscillator moves up through the midpoint line, it is considered to be bullish.

T   F   3. Extreme high oscillator readings are interpreted as prices reaching an overbought condition and generate an immediate sell signal.

T   F   4. A five-day momentum oscillator will rise if the price gains for the current day's activity is greater than the advance of five days ago.

T   F   5. Rate of change oscillators measure percentage change, while momentum oscillators measure point change.

T   F   6. Moving averages oscillators help to spot moving average crossovers.

Answers

1. *False.* Oscillators can be beneficial regardless of whether prices are moving up, down, or sideways.

2. *True.*

3. *False.* Oscillators can remain at extreme readings for lengthy periods of time. Therefore, extreme readings should be viewed as periods of market vulnerability and not as specific buy and sell signals.

4. *True.*

5. *True.*

6. *True.* When a moving average oscillator crosses the midpoint line, the two moving averages have crossed each other.

Relative Strength Index

The *Relative Strength Index* (RSI) is a price momentum indicator developed by J. Welles Wilder, Jr. Since its introduction in Wilder's 1978 book *New Concepts In Technical Trading Systems* (P.O. Box 128, McLeansville, NC 27301), it has become widely used by technicians, particularly those who are commodities and futures oriented.

RSI is frequently confused with relative strength analysis, which compares the performance of two items (such as, one stock with another or one stock with an overall market index). Its name is the only thing it has in common with relative strength analysis.

Conceptual Basis of the Relative Strength Index

Lesson 11 discussed rate of change oscillators. RSI is a rate of change oscillator. It measures the velocity at which prices are moving.

RSI was intentionally designed to address three flaws often associated with oscillators. First, at times, oscillators move erratically due to the drop off of old data in their calcualtion. For example, if one has a 10-day oscillator and 10 days ago the price of the security moved up or down dramatically, the current oscillator reading will be a misleading low or high reading. A second problem relates to the vertical scale for an oscillator. How high or low should the oscillator be to signal buying or selling opportunities? The third and final problem is the need to keep massive amounts of data for oscillator calculations. RSI presents a solution to these problems.

How to Calculate the Relative Strength Index

RSI is calculated as follows:

$$RSI = 100 - \frac{100}{1 + RS}$$

$$RS = \frac{\text{Average of N period's up closes}}{\text{Average of N period's down closes}}$$

N = number of periods used in the calculation

Let's use 14 days as an example. To get the average up value, add the total points gained on up days during the last 14 days and divide by 14. The average down value is arrived at by adding the total points lost on down days during the last 14 days and dividing by 14. Divide the average up value by the average down value to calculate RS. Insert the RS value into the formula and calculate the first day's RSI value.

Updating RSI each period is easy. Simply multiply the previous up and down average values by 13, add the latest day's gain or loss to the up or down average, and multiply the total by 14. Insert the new RS value into the RSI formula and recalculate RSI.

Table 12–1 shows a complete example of calculating RSI for 14 days. Wilder suggests the use of 14 days of data in the RSI calculation; however, other technicians have found that other time periods work with success as well.

In general, the greater the number of periods used, the more stable RSI is, and the fewer signals are generated. Short-term RSIs tend to produce more signals than longer-term RSIs, including more false signals.

Figure 12–1 compares RSIs of differing lengths — 9 and 14 days — for the Standard & Poor's 500 Index. Note the difference in the number of crossings of the 70 and 30 lines.

Interpreting the Relative Strength Index

RSI can be interpreted from the following five perspectives:

1. Extreme readings.
2. Chart patterns.
3. Failure swings.
4. Support and resistance.
5. Divergence.

Table 12-1
Example of How to Calculate the Relative Strength Index

Day	Closing price	Change in price from prior day Up	Down	Totals for last 14 days Up (A)	Down (B)	Averages for last 14 days (A)/14=(C) Up	(B)/14=(D) Down	Up average divided by down average (C)/(D)=(E)	1+(E)=(F)	100/(F)=(G)	RSI 100−(G)
1	43.000										
2	44.125	1.125									
3	43.250		0.875								
4	42.875		0.375								
5	43.000	0.125									
6	42.875		0.125								
7	42.625		0.250								
8	42.125		0.500								
9	42.750	0.625									
10	43.750	1.000									
11	44.125	0.375									
12	43.750		0.375								
13	44.500	0.750									
14	44.125		0.375	4.000	2.875	0.286	0.205	1.391	2.391	41.818	58.182
15	44.125			4.000	2.875	0.286	0.205	1.391	2.391	41.818	58.182
16	44.875	0.750		3.625	2.875	0.259	0.205	1.261	2.261	44.231	55.769
17	45.000	0.125		3.750	2.000	0.268	0.143	1.875	2.875	34.783	65.217
18	44.375		0.625	3.750	2.250	0.268	0.161	1.667	2.667	37.500	62.500
19	43.875		0.500	3.625	2.750	0.259	0.196	1.318	2.318	43.137	56.863
20	42.750		1.125	3.625	3.750	0.259	0.268	0.967	1.967	50.847	49.153
21	42.625		0.125	3.625	3.625	0.259	0.259	1.000	2.000	50.000	50.000
22	44.000	1.375		5.000	3.125	0.357	0.223	1.600	2.600	38.462	61.538
23	43.750		0.250	4.375	3.375	0.313	0.241	1.296	2.296	43.548	56.452

Table 12-1

Example of How To Calculate the Relative Strength Index (continued)

Day	Closing price	Change in price from prior day Up	Down	Totals for last 14 days Up (A)	Down (B)	Averages for last 14 days (A)/14=(C) Up	(B)/14=(D) Down	Up average divided by down average (C)/(D)=(E)	1+(E)=(F)	100/(F)=(G)	RSI 100-(G)
24	43.375		0.375	3.375	3.750	0.241	0.268	0.900	1.900	52.632	47.368
25	42.875		0.500	3.000	4.250	0.214	0.304	0.706	1.706	58.621	41.379
26	43.625	0.750		3.750	3.875	0.268	0.277	0.968	1.968	50.820	49.180
27	44.750	1.125		4.125	3.875	0.295	0.277	1.065	2.065	48.438	51.563
28	43.750		1.000	4.125	4.500	0.295	0.321	0.917	1.917	52.174	47.826
29	43.625		0.125	4.125	4.625	0.295	0.330	0.892	1.892	52.857	47.143
30	43.125		0.500	3.375	5.125	0.241	0.366	0.659	1.659	60.294	39.706
31	43.625	0.500		3.750	5.125	0.268	0.366	0.732	1.732	57.746	42.254
32	43.625			3.750	4.500	0.268	0.321	0.833	1.833	54.545	45.455
33	43.375		0.250	3.750	4.250	0.268	0.304	0.882	1.882	53.125	46.875
34	43.875	0.500		4.250	3.125	0.304	0.223	1.360	2.360	42.373	57.627
35	45.000	1.125		5.375	3.000	0.384	0.214	1.792	2.792	35.821	64.179
36	45.375	0.375		4.375	3.000	0.313	0.214	1.458	2.458	40.678	59.322
37	45.375			4.375	2.750	0.313	0.196	1.591	2.591	38.596	61.404
38	45.500	0.125		4.500	2.375	0.321	0.170	1.895	2.895	34.545	65.455
39	45.000		0.500	4.500	2.375	0.321	0.170	1.895	2.895	34.545	65.455
40	43.625		1.375	3.750	3.750	0.268	0.268	1.000	2.000	50.000	50.000
41	43.375		0.250	2.625	4.000	0.188	0.286	0.656	1.656	60.377	39.623
42	43.125		0.250	2.625	3.250	0.188	0.232	0.808	1.808	55.319	44.681
43	43.125			2.625	3.125	0.188	0.223	0.840	1.840	54.348	45.652
44	44.250	1.125		3.750	2.625	0.268	0.188	1.429	2.429	41.176	58.824
45	43.500		0.750	3.250	3.375	0.232	0.241	0.963	1.963	50.943	49.057
46	44.375	0.875		4.125	3.375	0.295	0.241	1.222	2.222	45.000	55.000
47	45.875	1.500		5.625	3.125	0.402	0.223	1.800	2.800	35.714	64.286
48	46.750	0.875		6.000	3.125	0.429	0.223	1.920	2.920	34.247	65.753
49	47.625	0.875		5.750	3.125	0.411	0.223	1.840	2.840	35.211	64.789
50	48.000	0.375		5.750	3.125	0.411	0.223	1.840	2.840	35.211	64.789

Figure 12–1
Comparison of Standard & Poor's 500 Index (Top), 9-Day Relative Strength Index (Middle), and 14-Day Relative Strength Index (Bottom)

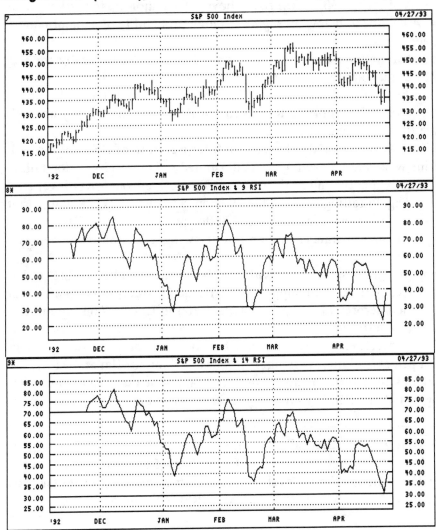

Let's examine each one in detail.

Extreme RSI readings signal the likelihood of major tops or bottoms. Although the exact levels to use are subject to debate, Wilder recommends using levels of 70 and 30. If RSI rises above 70, a major top in market prices is likely. A decline to below 30 suggests a high probability of a major bottom being made.

The chart patterns presented in Lessons 3 through 5 are equally applicable to RSI as they are to regular price charts. Often, chart patterns (such as a triangle or head and shoulders top or bottom) can be seen in RSI. Since the same breakout rules apply to RSI as to normal price charts, buy and sell points are frequently indicated.

Failure swings can also be used in interpretation of RSI. First of all, let's define what a failure swing is. As illustrated in Figure 12–2, a top failure swing occurs when the index rises above 70, declines to a lower level (fail point), rises again failing to reach the 70 level, and then falls below the prior lower level (a fail point). One would sell at that point.

Figure 12–3 illustrates a bottom failure swing. It is simply the opposite of a top failure swing.

Support and resistance lines will often be apparent on RSI before the bar chart of prices. Breaking of support or resistance is interpreted in a similar fashion to the interpretation of price charts. Refer to Lesson 7 on support and resistance for a refresher.

Finally, divergence between prices on a bar chart and RSI strongly suggests that prices will be reversing. If prices are rising or flat and RSI is decreasing, look for a turn downward in prices. If, on the other hand, prices are declining or flat and RSI is increasing, expect prices to turn and move higher.

TECHNICAL ANALYSIS TIP — A simple but effective method of interpreting RSI is to buy on the crossing up through the 50 level and sell on the crossing down through the 50 level. For overall stock market indexes (such as the Standard & Poor's 500 Index), a 21-week RSI is recommended.

Figure 12–2
Top Failure Swing

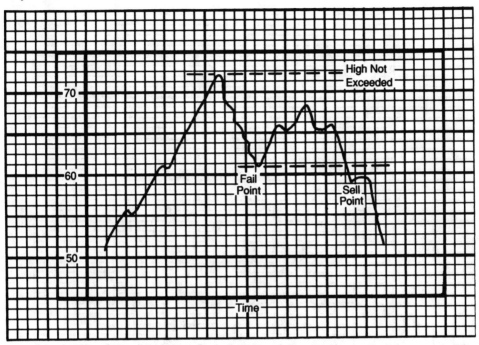

True or False Quiz

Circle T if the statement is true or F if the statement is false.

T   F   1. RSI is a rate of change oscillator.

T   F   2. Wilder suggests that when RSI rises above 70, it is bullish.

T   F   3. Chart patterns that appear on RSI charts should be interpreted in a similar manner to those appearing on bar charts.

T   F   4. Support and resistance lines will often become apparent on RSI before the bar chart of prices.

Figure 12–3
Bottom Failure Swing

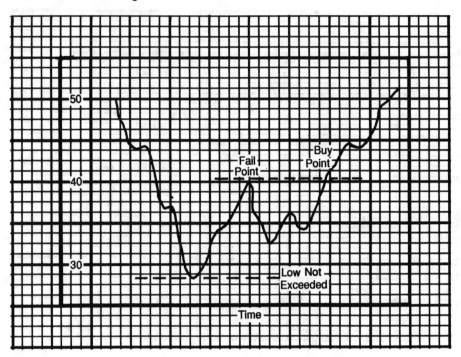

Answers

1. *True.*

2. *False.* If RSI rises above 70, a major top in market prices is likely. Therefore, it should be viewed as bearish.

3. *True.*

4. *True.*

Stochastics

The stochastics approach to market analysis was developed by George C. Lane (Investment Educators, 719 South Fourth Street, Watseka, IL 60970). It has become very popular among investors, especially those who are short-term oriented (although it is equally effective for longer investment horizons).

Stochastics is a price velocity technique based on the theory that as prices increase, closing prices have a tendency to be ever nearer to the highs for the period. Similarly, as prices move lower, closing prices tend to be closer and closer to the lows for the period.

Calculation

The formula for calculating stochastics is as follows:

$$\% \, K = \frac{(C - L)}{(H - L)} \times 100$$

where:

% K   is stochastics.
C   is the latest closing price.
L   is the low price during the last N periods.
H   is the high price during the last N periods.
N   can be any number of periods
      (Lane recommends using from 5 to 21 periods).

%K is then smoothed, typically using a three-period simple moving average, to derive %D.

The resulting %K and %D lines when plotted show, on a percentage basis of 0 to 100, where the closing price is relative to the range of prices for a given period of time (i.e., five days).

Stochastic calculations can be made and the indicator plotted by hand. However, if multiple securities are to be tracked, a lot of time can be saved by either subscribing to a chart service or, even better, by using a personal computer technical analysis software package.

An example of stochastics is provided in Figure 13–1. The upper half of the chart is a bar chart of the Standard & Poor's 500 Index. The bottom half is the stochastics plot. Note that the solid line represents %K and the dashed line is %D.

Divergence Analysis

The principal method of interpreting stochastics for buy and sell signals is through divergence analysis. A bearish divergence (see Figure 13–2) occurs when a security's price makes a high, then corrects moving lower, and subsequently reaches a higher high. At the same time, corresponding peaks of the %D line make a high followed by a lower high. Confirmation and the signal to sell occurs when the %K line moves below the %D line.

A bullish divergence (see Figure 13–3) occurs when a security's price makes a low, then corrects moving higher, and subsequently reaches a lower low. At the same time, corresponding bottoms of the %D line make a low followed by a lower low. Confirmation and the signal to buy comes when the %K line moves above the %D line.

TECHNICAL ANALYSIS TIP— Signals to buy and sell have a higher probability of success if they are given in the 10 percent to 15 percent range for buy signals (bullish divergences) and the 85 percent to 90 percent range for sell signals (bearish divergences).

Extreme Readings

It is not unusual for the %K line to reach 0 or 100 percent. These readings do not mean that the price of a particular security has reached a bottom (0 per-

**Figure 13–1
Standard & Poor's 500 Index (Top)
versus Five-Day Stochastics Plot (Bottom)**

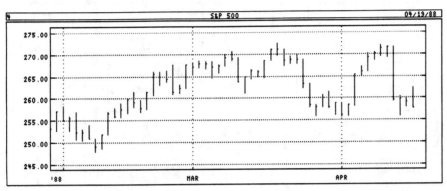

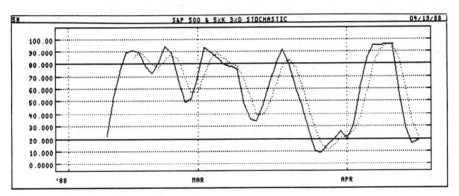

cent) or top (100 percent). It does suggest great weakness (0 percent) or strength (100 percent).

When a reading of 0 percent is reached, the %K line frequently moves up to the 20–25 percent level and then declines again to or near the 0 percent level. When %K moves up from that area, one can expect a minor rally in prices to occur.

The opposite holds true for 100 percent readings. After reaching 100 percent, the %K line often will drop to the 75–80 percent range and then move back up to or near the 100 percent level. On the %K line's next decline, a minor reaction (drop in prices) is likely.

Figure 13–2
Example of a Bearish Divergence

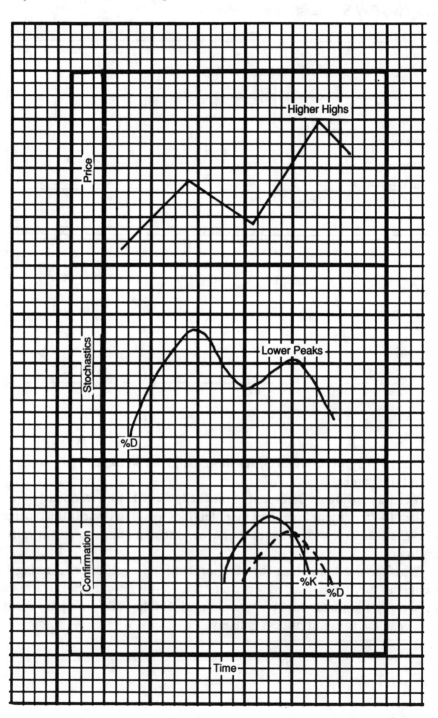

Figure 13–3
Example of a Bullish Divergence

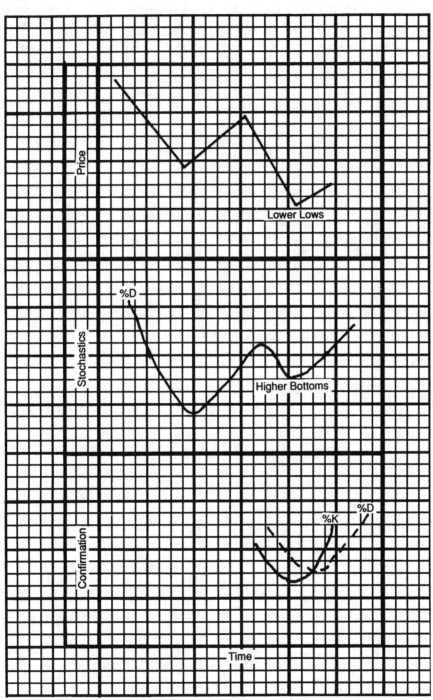

Reversal Warning Signal

When the %K line has been moving in one direction for many periods and suddenly, one period reverses direction sharply (for 2 to 12 percent), a warning signal is given. Prices are likely to reverse direction in one or two periods.

True or False Quiz

Circle T if the statement is true or F if the statement is false.

T   F   1. The stochastics approach is only effective for short-term analysis.

T   F   2. Stochastics is based on the theory that as prices increase (or decrease), closing prices have a tendency to be closer and closer to the highs (or lows) for the period.

T   F   3. Divergence analysis is the principal method of using stochastics to generate buy and sell signals.

T   F   4. A %K line reading of 0 percent means that the price of a security has reached a bottom.

Answers

1. *False.* The stochastics approach is equally as effective for long-term analysis as it is for the short-term.

2. *True.*

3. *True.*

4. *False.* A %K line reading of 0 percent implies great weakness, not that the price of a security has reached a bottom.

ALTERNATIVE CHARTING METHODS

Point and Figure Charting

Although not used as widely as bar charts, *point and figure charts* have been around since the late 1800s. This lesson will show how to construct and interpret point and figure charts.

Point and Figure Charts versus Bar Charts

Bar charts are by far the most popular type of charts used by technicians. In addition to bar charts, a significant number of technicians use point and figure charts to track market action.

What are the differences between point and figure charts and bar charts? There are two main ones.

First, visually the two types of charts look different. Figure 14–1 shows a daily point and figure chart of Hewlett Packard for a one year period. Figure 14–2 provides a bar chart of Hewlett Packard for the same time period.

By examining the horizontal axis on each chart, one notes that the time periods are evenly spaced out on the bar chart, but not on the point and figure chart. Point and figure charts are simply a study of price action. Time is not taken into consideration when prices are plotted.

A second difference relates to the recording of volume. Bar charts often include a volume histogram at the bottom of the chart (see Figure 14–2). Point and figure charts do not include a volume histogram or other graphic representation of volume activity. However, some technicians argue that volume is reflected in the number of price changes shown on the chart.

Figure 14–1
Point and Figure Chart for Hewlett Packard

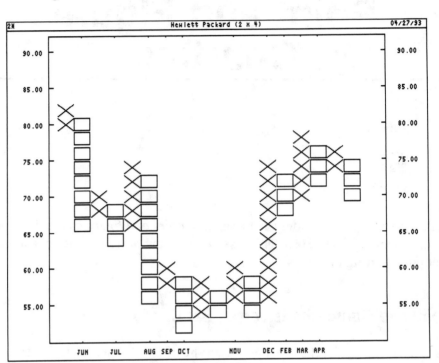

Constructing Point and Figure Charts

Box size and reversal criteria are two items that must be determined before constructing a point and figure chart.

Box Size

Box size is simply the value of each box on the chart. On a relative basis, the smaller the box size, the more sensitive to price movements the chart will be. For example, each box could represent one dollar of price movement. A more sensitive chart could be produced using a box size of $.50 or $.25. On the other hand, a box size of three dollars could be used to generate a less sensitive chart.

Figures 14–3 and 14–4 show the same data for Eastman Kodak using one-half and one dollar box sizes, respectively. Note that the smaller box size

Figure 14–2
Bar Chart for Hewlett Packard

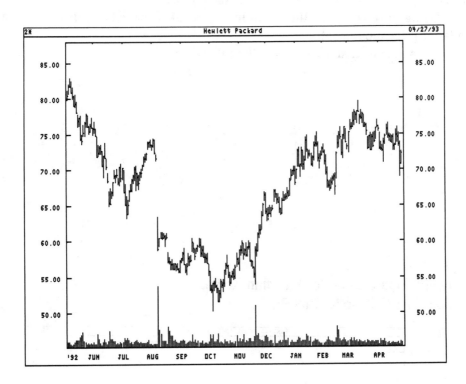

results in more boxes being used and a shorter-term perspective than that generated using the larger box size.

Reversal Criteria

The *reversal criteria* can be defined as the number of boxes required to be retraced to cause a reversal and, thus, the recording of prices in the next column in the opposite direction. For example, a three box reversal method is often used. As illustrated in Figure 14–5, a three box reversal requires that three boxes be retraced before a reversal is signaled. In Figure 14–5, each box represents one dollar of price movement; therefore three dollars of price movement must be retraced for a reversal to occur.

A one box reversal for the same data is shown in Figure 14–6. Note that reversals are more frequent, and longer-term price trends are more difficult to discern.

Once box size and reversal criteria have been determined, construction of a point and figure chart is easy. For illustrative purposes, let's use a one dollar box size and a reversal criteria of three boxes.

Using grid paper, as illustrated in Figure 14–7, each box represents one dollar of price movement.

Let's assume a stock trades at the following prices:

Period	Price
1	22
2	23
3	23½
4	24
5	25
6	27
7	26
8	24
9	23

Figure 14–3
Point and Figure Chart for Eastman Kodak
Using a One-Half Dollar Box Size

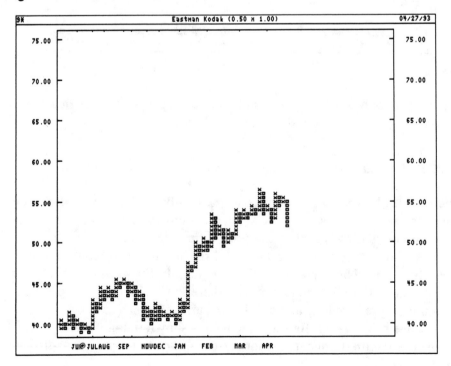

Figure 14–4
Point and Figure Chart for Eastman Kodak
Using a One Dollar Box Size

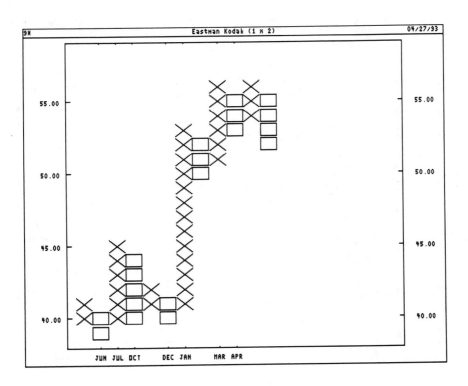

The first price, or X, representing up price movement, would be placed in the $22 box. Since prices moved up through $27, each box up through $27 would be filled with an X. During period 7, the price dropped from $27 to $26. However, since the reversal criteria is three boxes, nothing is plotted. The reversal criteria is met in period 8. Thus a 0 (representing down price movement) is placed in the $24 box in the next column. In the following period, the price dropped to $23, and another 0 is plotted.

Figure 14-5
Point and Figure Chart for Eastman Kodak
Using a Three Box Reversal

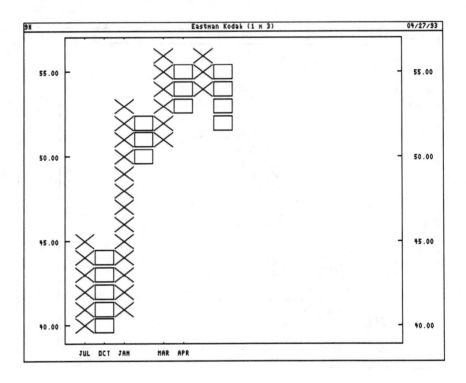

TECHNICAL ANALYSIS TIP — Should you use intraday or daily price data? Pure point and figure chartists contend that point and figure charts should reflect all price activity occuring during the day and not just the closing price or low to high price range for the day. Some reversals will appear using intraday data that will not show on charts using low to high price range data. However, most investors have neither access to intraday, trade by trade data nor the time to plot it.

From a practical point of view the benefits of using intraday data are probably exceeded by the costs of obtaining and recording such information. It is suggested that you use the more readily available information, but recognize that from a pure point of view, all reversals may not be shown.

Figure 14–6
Point and Figure Chart for Eastman Kodak
Using a One Box Reversal

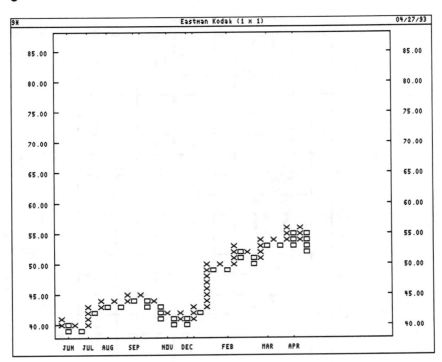

Chart Patterns

Just as with bar charts, chart patterns appear with enough frequency on point and figure charts to warrant watching for them. Head and shoulders and other chart patterns are similar to those associated with bar charts.

Trendlines

Trendlines can be drawn on point and figure charts just as they are drawn on bar charts. Up trendlines can be drawn by connecting lows, and down trend-lines can be drawn by connecting highs. Interpretation of trendline breaks is the same as with bar charts.

Figure 14–7
Example of Constructing a Point and Figure Chart
with a One Dollar Box Size and Three Box Reversal Criteria

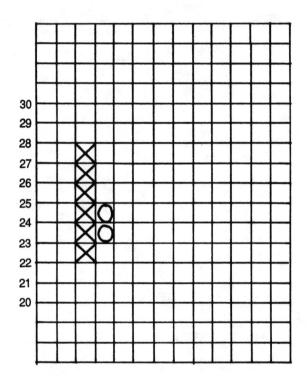

Similarly, support and resistance lines, trend channel lines, and many other technical tools are equally valid on point and figure charts as they are on bar charts.

True or False Quiz

Circle T if the statement is true or F if the statement is false.

T   F   1. Time periods are evenly spaced on the horizontal axis of both bar charts and point and figure charts.

T   F   2. The box size and reversal criteria must be determined before you can construct a point and figure chart.

T   F   3. The smaller the box size, the more sensitive to price movements the chart will be.

T   F   4. A head and shoulders top chart pattern on a point and figure chart should not be interpreted the same as a head and shoulders top chart pattern on a bar chart.

T   F   5. Trendlines, support and resistance lines, and many other technical tools are as valid on point and figure charts as they are on bar charts.

Answers

1. *False.* Time periods are evenly spaced out on bar charts but not on point and figure charts.

2. *True.*

3. *True.*

4. *False.* As with many chart patterns, interpretation of the head and shoulders top is the same on both a bar chart and a point and figure chart.

5. *True.*

Japanese Candlestick Charting

Although candlestick charting has been used by Japanese traders for centuries, it has only recently captured the attention of Wall Street. This lesson will show you how to construct and interpret candlestick charts.

Before continuing, let's visually compare a candlestick chart to a bar chart. Figure 15–1 presents a standard bar chart. Figure 15–2 plots the same data in candlestick chart form. As can readily be seen, the two charting methods have many similarities. First, the scaling is the same. Second, the overall shape of the charts is the same. Third, both charts can be used in conjunction with other technical analysis tools (i.e., moving averages, oscillators, etc.). Fourth, the high-low range for each period is the same. Basically, the only difference is how the opening and closing prices are shown.

Constructing Candlestick Lines

Candlestick lines are easy to construct. Each line represents the trading activity for one period (i.e., hour, day, week, month, etc.) and shows opening, high, low, and closing prices.

The main body (the thick part) of the candlestick line represents the range between the period's opening and closing prices. If the closing price is higher than the opening price, the main body is white (empty). On the other hand, if the closing price is lower than the opening price, the main body is black (filled in).

Figure 15–1
Example of Bar Chart

Figure 15–2
Example of Japanese Candlestick Chart

The thin lines above and below the main body are called shadows. They show the high and low prices for the period (in a similar fashion to bar charts).

Figure 15–3 presents a long white body. This is considered bullish since prices closed near the high of the period after trading in a wide range.

Figure 15–4 illustrates a long black body. This is viewed as bearish since prices traded within a wide range and closed near the low of the period.

There can be periods in which the body is neither white nor black. This occurs when the opening and closing prices for a period are the same; it is known as a doji line.

Since the opening price is required for each period, candlestick charting is limited, from a practical point of view, in its usefulness to futures and commodities. Opening prices for stocks are not readily available to most investors. Although some quotation services do provide opening prices, they are not published in financial newspapers or typically available for downloading from an on-line database to a technical analysis software package. However, this does not entirely preclude stock market investors from taking advantage

Figure 15–3
Long White Body

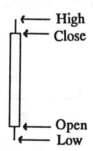

Figure 15–4
Long Black Body

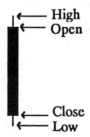

of candlestick charting. For example, the Standard & Poor's 500 Index futures contract could be plotted as a substitute for the Standard & Poor's 500 Index and used to monitor the direction of the overall stock market.

Candlestick lines can take a variety of shapes depending upon the relationship of the period's opening, high, low, and closing prices. Figure 15–5 presents the more common shapes along with their interpretation.

As with bar charts, patterns can develop in candlestick charts that help forecast the future direction of prices. For purposes of discussion, we have divided the primary candlestick chart patterns into three types — bullish reversal, bearish reversal, and continuation.

Bullish reversal patterns are considered to be legitimate if formed after prices have been in a downtrend. Bearish reversal patterns appearing after an uptrend in prices are viewed as valid. Continuation patterns can occur in both upward and downward movements in prices.

Key Bullish Reversal Patterns

Hammer (see Figure 15–6): A hammer occurs when prices rally from an intra-period sell-off to close near the open. This results in the main body, which can be either black or white, being at the upper end of the period's trading

Figure 15–5
Various Candlestick Lines

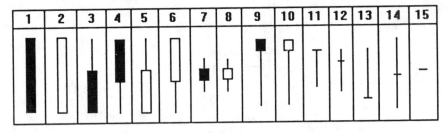

Interpretation

1. Extremely bearish
2. Extremely bullish
3. Bearish
4. Bearish
5. Bullish
6. Bullish
7. Neutral
8. Neutral

9. In downtrend, bullish; in uptrend, bearish
10. In downtrend, bullish; in uptrend, bearish
11. A turning period
12. A turning period
13. End of downtrend
14. A turning period
15. Possible turning period

Figure 15–6
Hammer

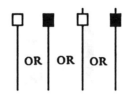

range with little or no upper shadow. The lower shadow must be at least twice the length of the main body for the pattern to be considered legitimate.

Bullish Engulfing Pattern (see Figure 15–7): A bullish engulfing pattern occurs when prices open lower than the previous period's close and then rally to close above the previous period's open. Thus, the current period's white main body engulfs the prior period's black main body. You should note that only the main body is important in this pattern; both upper and lower shadows are ignored.

Tweezer Bottom (see Figure 15–8): A tweezer bottom pattern is simply two consecutive periods with matching lows. It isn't important whether the candle lines have white or black main bodies (or are simply doji lines). There are no requirements regarding the length of upper and lower shadow lines. All that matters is that the lows for the two periods are the same.

Piercing Line (see Figure 15–9): A piercing line pattern occurs when prices gap lower on the opening and then retrace to close above the midpoint of the previous period's black body. This results in a period having a black main body being followed by a period with a white main body and, in the

Figure 15–7
Bullish Engulfing Pattern

Figure 15–8
Tweezer Bottom

Figure 15–9
Piercing Line

second period, (1) the open is lower than the previous period's low and (2) the close is higher than the center of the previous period's black main body.

   Morning Star (see Figure 15–10): A morning star pattern develops over three periods. In the first period, prices close lower than they opened resulting in a black main body. In the second period, prices open lower creating a

Figure 15–10
Morning Star

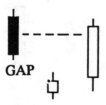

GAP

downside gap and close higher after trading in a relatively narrow range (a small main body). Finally, in the third period, prices continue to move higher and close above the midpoint of the first period's black main body.

Bullish Doji Star (see Figure 15–11): A bullish doji star pattern occurs when prices gap to the downside on the open and then close at the same price as the open.

Bullish Harami (see Figure 15–12): A harami pattern is similar to an inside period. The open to close range (main body) for the current period falls within the open to close range (main body) of the previous period. Note that it doesn't matter whether the main bodies for the two periods are both black, both white, or one is black and one is white. What is important is when the pattern occurs. If a harami pattern occurs in a downtrend, it is considered a bullish reversal signal.

Bullish Harami Cross (see Figure 15–13): The harami cross pattern is the same as the harami chart formation except that the open and close are the same in the second period. If a harami cross pattern occurs in a downtrend, it is viewed as a bullish reversal signal.

Figure 15–11
Bullish Doji Star

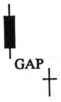

GAP

Figure 15–12
Bullish Harami

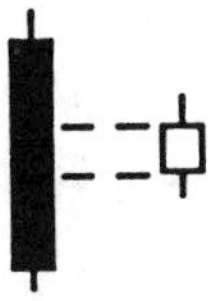

Figure 15–13
Bullish Harami Cross

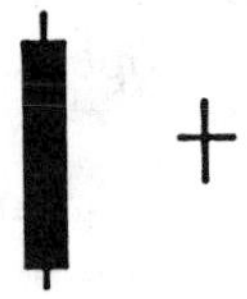

Bullish Meeting Lines (see Figure 15–14): A bullish meeting lines pattern occurs when prices gap lower on the open and close unchanged from the previous period. A black main body in the first period is followed by a white main body in the second period.

Key Bearish Reversal Patterns

Hanging Man (see Figure 15–15): A hanging man occurs when prices rally from an intra-period sell-off to close near the open. This results in the main body, which can be either black or white, being at the upper end of the period's trading range with little or no upper shadow. The lower shadow must be at least twice the length of the main body for the pattern to be considered legitimate. Note that the only difference between a hanging man and a hammer is when the pattern occurs on the chart. If it develops after an uptrend in prices, it is a hanging man. If it forms after a downtrend in prices, it is a ham-

Figure 15–14
Bullish Meeting Lines

Figure 15–15
Hanging Man

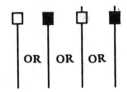

mer. Regardless of whether you call the pattern a hanging man or a hammer, it signals a reversal in the trend of prices.

Bearish Engulfing Pattern (see Figure 15–16): A bearish engulfing pattern occurs when prices open higher than the previous period's close and then sell-off to close below the previous period's open. Thus, the current period's black main body engulfs the prior period's white main body. You should note that only the main body is important in this pattern; both upper and lower shadows are ignored.

Tweezer Top (see Figure 15–17): A tweezer top pattern is simply consecutive periods with matching highs. It isn't important whether the candle lines have white or black main bodies (or are simply doji lines). There are no requirements regarding the length of upper and lower shadow lines. All that matters is that the highs for the two periods are the same.

Dark Cloud Cover (see Figure 15–18): A dark cloud cover pattern occurs when prices gap higher on the opening and then retrace to close below the midpoint of the previous period's black body. This results in a period hav-

Figure 15–16
Bearish Engulfing Pattern

Figure 15–17
Tweezer Top

Figure 15–18
Dark Cloud Cover

ing a white main body being followed by a period with a black main body and, in the second period, (1) the open is higher than the previous period's high and (2) the close is lower than the center of the previous period's white main body.

   Upside Gap Two Crows (see Figure 15–19): An upside gap two crows pattern forms when prices meet resistance on two consecutive days after gapping higher. A period having a white main body is followed by two periods with black main bodies. There is an upside gap between the white main body and the first black main body.

   Evening Star (see Figure 15–20): An evening star pattern develops over three periods. In the first period, prices close higher than they open resulting in a white main body. In the second period, prices open higher creating an upside gap and close lower after trading in a relatively narrow range (a small main body). Finally, in the third period, prices continue to move lower and close below the midpoint of the first period's white main body.

Figure 15–19
Upside Gap Two Crows

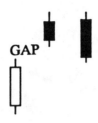

Figure 15–20
Evening Star

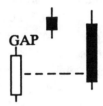

Bearish Doji Star (see Figure 15–21): A bearish doji star pattern occurs when prices gap to the upside on the open and then close at the same price as the open.

Shooting Star (see Figure 15–22): A shooting star pattern is simply a period having a small main body, which can be either black or white, at the lower end of the price range with a long upper shadow.

Figure 15–21
Bearish Doji Star

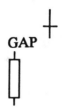

Figure 15–22
Shooting Star

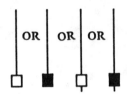

Bearish Harami (see Figure 15–23): A harami pattern is similar to an inside period. The open to close range (main body) for the current period falls within the open to close range (main body) of the previous period. Note that it doesn't matter whether the main bodies for the two periods are both black, both white, or one is black and one is white. What is important is when the pattern occurs. If a harami pattern occurs in an uptrend, it is considered a bearish reversal signal.

Bearish Harami Cross (see Figure 15–24): The harami cross pattern is the same as the harami chart formation except that the open and close are the same in the second period. If a harami cross pattern occurs in an uptrend, it is viewed as a bearish reversal signal.

Bearish Meeting Lines (see Figure 15–25): A bearish meeting lines pattern occurs when prices gap higher on the open and then close unchanged from the previous period. A white main body in the first period is followed by a black main body in the second period.

Figure 15–23
Bearish Harami

Figure 15–24
Bearish Harami Cross

Figure 15–25
Bearish Meeting Lines

Key Continuation Patterns

Window (see Figure 15–26): A window is simply a gap (an area on a chart where no actual trading takes place). Gaps frequently act as support or resistance. An upside window (gap) is considered to be bullish, while a downside window (gap) is viewed as bearish.

Upside Tasuki Gap (see Figure 15–27): An upside tasuki gap pattern develops over three periods. In the first period, prices close above their open resulting in a white main body. In the second period, prices gap to the upside on the open and then close higher (creating a white main body). In the third period, prices open within the main body of the second period and then close lower, but do not fill the gap (with either the main body or the lower shadow). This suggests that only a temporary setback has occurred and that prices will continue higher (in essence, because the gap has acted as a support level).

Figure 15–26
Window

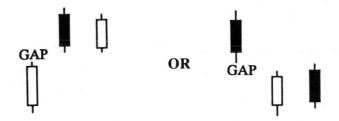

Figure 15–27
Upside Tasuki Gap

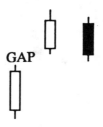

Rising Three Methods (see Figure–28): A rising three methods pattern occurs when a long white main body is followed by three or more small white or black main bodies and then a long white main body which makes a new high close for the move. It is similar to a flag pattern on a bar chart and typically appears after a dynamic rally. It represents some profit-taking before the rally continues.

Falling Three Methods (see Figure 15–29): A falling three methods pattern occurs when a long black body is followed by three or more small white or black main bodies and then a long black main body which makes a new low close for the move. It is similar to a flag pattern on a bar chart and typically appears after a sharp downtrend. It represents short-covering before the drop in prices continues.

Side-by-Side White Lines (Upside Gap) (see Figure 15–30): This pattern develops over three periods. In the first period, the main body can be either white or black. Prices gap to the upside on the opening of the second period and then close higher. In the third period, prices open at the same opening

Figure 15–28
Rising Three Methods

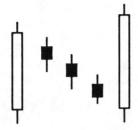

Figure 15–29
Falling Three Methods

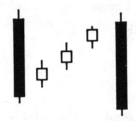

Figure 15–30
Side-by-Side White Lines (Upside Gap)

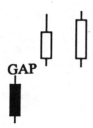

price as in the second period and close higher. The inability of prices to fill the gap indicates a strong support level.

Side-by-Side White Lines (Downside Gap) (see Figure 15–31): This pattern develops over three periods. In the first period, the main body can be either white or black. Prices gap to the downside on the opening of the sec-

Figure 15–31
Side-by-Side White Lines (Downside Gap)

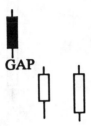

ond period and then close higher. In the third period, prices close at the same closing price as in the second period after having risen from the open. The inability of prices to fill the gap indicates a strong resistance level.

Real Market Examples

Real market examples of several candlestick chart patterns are shown in Figures 15–32 (Standard & Poor's 500 Index Futures) and 15–33 (Treasury Bond Futures). Note that not all candlestick chart patterns are highlighted. Further study of each chart will result in identification of additional candlestick chart patterns, as well as notation of their predictive value.

Figure 15–32
Standard & Poor's 500 Index Futures Contract

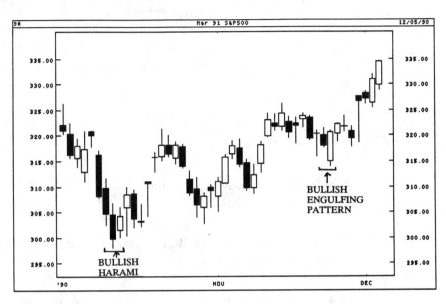

Figure 15–33
Treasury Bond Futures Contract

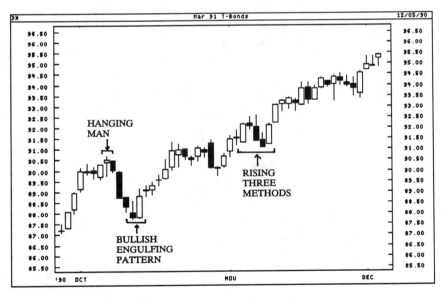

True or False Quiz

Circle T if the statement is true or F if the statement is false.

T   F   1. The opening price, along with high, low, and closing prices for each period are required in order to prepare candlestick charts.

T   F   2. Candlestick charts more closely resemble bar charts than point and figure charts.

T   F   3. Trendlines and moving averages are typically not used with candlestick charts.

T   F   4. The main body of the candlestick line represents the range between the period's high and low prices.

T   F   5. A hammer pattern looks the same as a hanging man pattern.

T   F   6. A doji line occurs when the opening and closing prices for a period are the same.

Answers

1. *True.*

2. *True.*

3. *False.* Many technical analysis tools (including trendlines and moving averages) are commonly used in conjunction with candlestick charts.

4. *False.* The main body of the candlestick line represents the range between the period's opening and closing prices.

5. *True.*

6. *True.*

OVERALL MARKET ANALYSIS

The Dow Theory

The *Dow Theory* is one of the oldest and most famous technical theories on how to determine the major trend of prices in the stock market. The basic principles of the theory were originated by Charles H. Dow, the founder of Dow Jones and Company, and first appeared in the late 1800s in a series of editorials in the *Wall Street Journal.* During the early 1900s, William P. Hamilton (Dow's successor as editor of the *Wall Street Journal*) organized those basic principles into what became known as The Dow Theory.

The Dow Theory assumes that most stocks move in conjunction with the overall market. If the stock market moves up, the vast majority of stocks move up. Likewise, if the stock market moves down, most stocks move in sympathy to the downside.

To represent the overall market, Dow devised two market indexes, namely, the Industrial Average and the Rail Average. These indexes have evolved over time and are now called the Dow Jones Industrial Average and the Dow Jones Transportation Average.

The Dow Jones Industrial Average currently comprises 30 major industrial corporations, such as General Electric, General Motors, and International Business Machines. The Dow Jones Transportation Average includes 20 transportation companies, such as Consolidated Freight, Federal Express, and Union Pacific. Each index is used by The Dow Theory.

Figure 16–1 presents a comparison of the Dow Jones Industrial Average to the Dow Jones Transportation Average for two years. Note how they move in tandem most of the time.

Figure 16–1
Dow Jones Industrial Average (Top)
versus Dow Jones Transportation Average (Bottom)

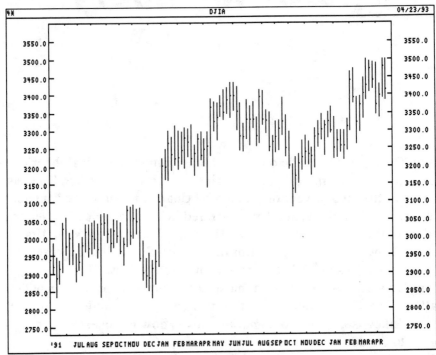

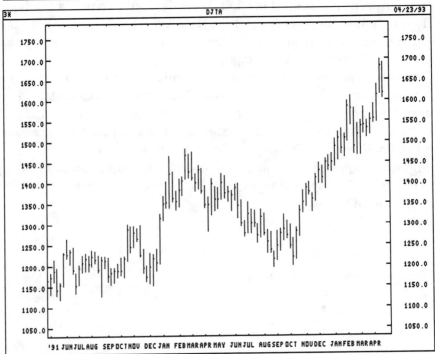

Basic Principles

The Dow Theory is based upon numerous tenets or principles. A discussion of each of the seven essential principles follows.

1. The averages discount everything.   Lesson 1 taught that one of the principles of technical analysis is that the market discounts everything (all information—economic, fundamental, psychological, etc.). That concept originates with The Dow Theory in which Dow noted that since the averages (and, in particular, the Dow Jones Industrial Average and the Dow Jones Transportation Average) reflect the activities of all stock market investors, everything that could possibly affect the supply and demand balance for stocks is discounted by the averages.

2. There are three trends in the market, namely, primary trends, secondary reactions, and minor trends.   Primary trends represent the long-term trend in the price of stocks. Secondary reactions interrupt and act in the opposite direction of the primary trend and are considered to be corrective in nature. Minor trends are day-to-day fluctuations. Minor trends are disregarded in The Dow Theory.

In order to explain the three trend types, Dow used analogies to the movements of the sea. The primary trend is like the tide; secondary reactions are similar to waves; and hourly or daily fluctuations compare to ripples. All three movements occur simultaneously.

3. Primary uptrends usually have three up moves.   Primary uptrends are normally called bull markets and consist of three moves up in stock prices. The first move up results from far-sighted investors accumulating stocks at a time when business is slow but anticipated to improve. Investors buying stocks based on increased company earnings causes the second move up. The final move up occurs when all the financial news is good. This final move is accompanied by rampant speculation.

4. Primary downtrends usually have three down moves.   Primary downtrends are normally called bear markets and consist of three moves down in stock prices. The first move down occurs when far-sighted investors sell stocks recognizing that business earnings have reached a level too high to be maintained. The second down move reflects panic as buyers become scarce and sellers rush to get out of the market. The final move down results from distress selling and the need to raise cash.

5. To signal a bull or bear trend, the two averages must confirm each other.
To signal a bull trend, both the Dow Jones Industrial Average and the Dow Jones Transportation Average must rise above their respective highs of previous upward secondary reactions. To signal a bear trend, both averages must drop below their respective lows of previous secondary reactions. Normally, one average will indicate a change in the trend, either from bull to bear or bear to bull, before the other. The other average must also reach the appropriate price level to indicate a change in trend for The Dow Theory signal to be given. However, The Dow Theory stipulates no time period beyond which a confirmation becomes invalid.

Figure 16–2 shows a hypothetical chart of a confirmation of the two averages. Note that at point A the Dow Jones Industrial Average reaches a new high after a secondary downside reaction and generates a bull trend signal. The signal is subsequently confirmed by the Dow Jones Transportation Average at point B.

Figure 16–3 illustrates a failure by one average (in this example, the Dow Jones Transportation Average) to confirm a signal generated by the other average (in this example, The Dow Jones Industrial Average). As a result of the lack of confirmation, a bull trend signal is not given by The Dow Theory.

6. Only closing prices are used. The Dow Theory signals are generated using closing prices only. Daily high and low prices are not considered.

7. A trend remains effective until a reversal has been signaled by both averages.

The Dow Theory's Defects

Since its introduction in the late 1800s, The Dow Theory has been very successful. Nonetheless, it is criticized for several reasons.

A major criticism of The Dow Theory is that it is frequently late in giving signals. Thus, it deprives investors of profits that could be earned during the beginning and end of major moves. For example, the inception of a bull market is not signaled until the market breaks above the previous secondary tops in both averages. This means buying is done on powerful up movements.

Figure 16–2
Hypothetical Chart of a Confirmation of the Two Averages

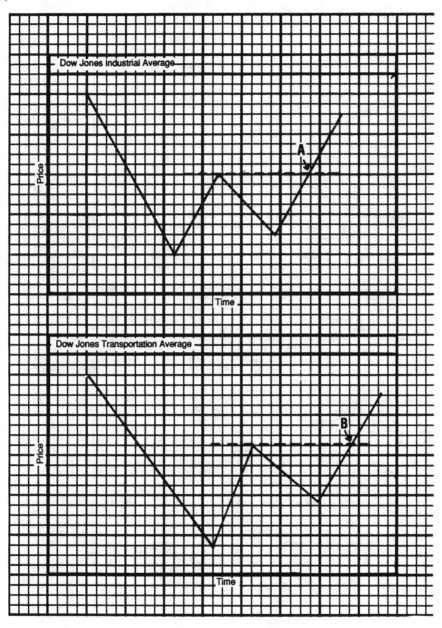

Figure 16–3
Hypothetical Chart of One Average's Failure
to Confirm the Other Average

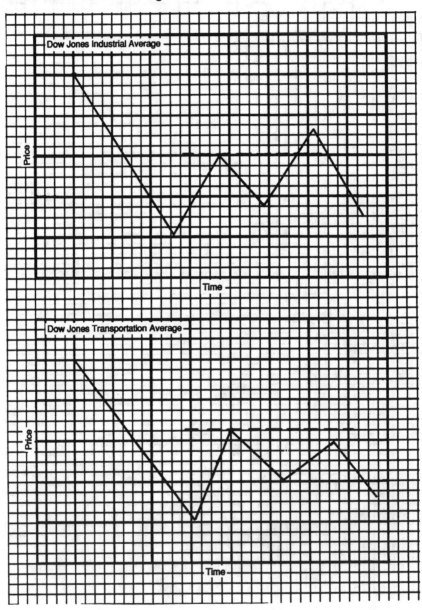

Likewise, after a bear trend signal, selling is done on the collapse in prices well below the tops.

In that regard, The Dow Theory is like the vast majority of trend following techniques, which does not identify the emergence of a major bull or bear trend until it has made a significant move (typically, 20 to 30 percent).

Some critics of The Dow Theory argue that it is very vague because it does not precisely define what the duration and extent should be for primary, secondary, and minor trends. At times, this results in followers of The Dow Theory disagreeing about the direction of the primary trend because of differences in interpretation.

A third criticism of The Dow Theory is that it does not give intermediate- or short-term trend signals and, thus, does not help those types of investors. This is true, but its originator, Charles Dow, had no intention that it should be used in such fashion. It was designed to determine the primary trend of market prices only.

Finally, The Dow Theory is not infallible. It has given several bad signals. However, historically the losses resulting from such signals have been very small relative to the profits that could have been made from the eight times as many good signals.

Regardless of what the critics say, the record speaks for itself. For the 90-year period beginning in 1897, The Dow Theory gave 40 correct signals and only 5 wrong signals (4 of which resulted in losses of 7 percent or less).

True or False Quiz

Circle T if the statement is true or F if the statement is false.

T   F   1. The Dow Theory uses both the Dow Jones Industrial Average and the Dow Jones Utility Average.

T   F   2. The Dow Theory assumes there are three trends in the market, namely, primary, secondary, and minor trends.

T   F   3. Secondary trends are in the same direction as primary trends.

T   F   4. Minor trends are equally as important as secondary trends in The Dow Theory.

T   F   5. Primary downtrends usually have four down moves.

T   F   6. To signal a bull trend, only one of either the Dow Jones Industrial Average or the Dow Jones Transportation Average must rise above its high of the preceding upward secondary reaction.

T   F   7. Confirmation of a signal given by the Dow Jones Industrial Average must be made by the Dow Jones Transportation Average within three months, or the signal is withdrawn.

T   F   8. The Dow Theory frequently gives signals only after the market has moved significantly from a major top or bottom.

T   F   9. The Dow Theory has never given a bad signal.

Answers

1. *False.* The Dow Theory uses both the Dow Jones Industrial Average and the Dow Jones Transportation Average, but not the Dow Jones Utility Average.

2. *True.*

3. *False.* Secondary reactions (trends) interrupt and act in the opposite direction of the primary trend.

4. *False.* Secondary trends are an important component of The Dow Theory, while minor trends are disregarded.

5. *False.* Primary downtrends usually have three down moves.

6. *False.* Both averages must rise above their respective highs of previous upward secondary reactions. See Figure 16–2.

7. *False.* No time period is stipulated by The Dow Theory beyond which a confirmation becomes invalid.

8. *True.* Since a bull or bear market is not signaled until the market breaks above or below the previous secondary tops or bottoms in both averages, the market normally has already moved significantly from a major top or bottom.

9. *False.* It has given several bad (unprofitable) signals. However, the ratio of good (profitable) to bad signals is about eight to one.

Technical Market Indicators

It is widely recognized that most stocks move in the same direction as the overall stock market. If the market is moving up, the majority of stocks will move up; if the market is moving down, most stocks will move lower. Because of this correlation, most technicians believe that determining the trend of the overall stock market is essential to successful investing.

Over the years, a large body of technical market indicators has been developed to help evaluate the overall trend of the stock market. These technical market indicators are normally divided into three types, which are called breadth, sentiment, and monetary.

Breadth Indicators

Breadth indicators show market strength and weakness. They include advance/decline, volume, and new high/new low indicators. Let's examine several of these indicators in detail.

Advance/Decline Indicators

Advance-Decline Line

How to Calculate:

Each period, calculate the difference between the number of advancing issues and the number of declining issues and add that difference to the previous period's running total. Daily or weekly New York Stock Exchange data are typically used in the calculation.

The trend of the Advance-Decline Line is more important than its actual value. Therefore, you can begin its calculation at any point in time. However, you should use a large base number when you start (+50,000 is recommended) to avoid negative number readings when there is a decline in prices over a long period of time. An example of the indicator's calculation follows:

Base Number Day	Number of Advancing Issues	Number of Declining Issues	Difference	Value of Advance-Decline Line
				50,000
1	390	810	-420	49,580
2	580	620	- 40	49,540
3	750	520	+230	49,770
4	900	405	+495	50,265
5	580	640	- 60	50,205

How to Interpret:

The Advance-Decline Line is designed to facilitate comparison to a market index, such as the Standard & Poor's 500 Index. Interpretation of the Advance-Decline Line is commonly performed as follows:

Market Index	Advance-Decline Line	Interpretation
Rising	Falling	Bearish
Near or at previous top	Significantly below corresponding top	Bearish
Near or at previous top	Significantly above corresponding top	Bullish
Falling	Rising	Bullish
Near or at previous bottom	Significantly above previous bottom	Bullish
Near or at previous bottom	Significantly below previous bottom	Bearish

Chart Example:
Figure 17–1 provides a comparison of the Advance-Decline Line versus the Standard & Poor's 500 Index.

TECHNICAL ANALYSIS TIP — Don't rely on just one technical market indicator for buy and sell signals. Even the most reliable indicators are wrong frequently enough to warrant examination of several indicators to gain a consensus opinion of the probable direction of stock market prices.

Advance/Decline Noncumulative

How to Calculate:
The Advance/Decline Noncumulative is calculated in two steps. First, subtract the number of declining issues from the number of advancing issues. Second, divide the calculated number by the total number of issues traded.

Figure 17–1
Advance-Decline Line (Top)
versus the Standard & Poor's 500 Index (Bottom)

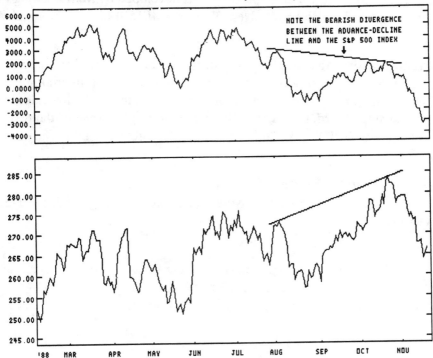

Daily or weekly New York Stock Exchange data are typically used in the calculation.

How to Interpret:
    Daily and weekly readings provide little guidance unless they are smoothed by a moving average. A 10-period simple moving average is suggested, and when used, should be interpreted as follows:

Period	Type of Moving Average	Bullish Readings	Bearish Readings
Daily	10-Day Simple	Over +0.08	Under -0.2
Weekly	10-Week Simple	Over +0.14	Under -0.2

Chart Example:
    Figure 17–2 provides a comparison of a 10-day simple moving average of the Advance/Decline Noncumulative versus the Standard & Poor's 500 Index.

Breadth Advance/Decline Indicator

The Breadth Advance/Decline Indicator was developed by Martin Zweig (The Zweig Forecast, P.O. Box 5345, New York, NY 10150).

How to Calculate:
    The Breadth Advance/Decline Indicator is calculated in three steps. First, add the number of advancing issues to the number of declining issues. Second, divide the number of advancing issues by the sum of the calculation in the first step. Third, take a 10-day simple moving average of the result of step two. New York Stock Exchange data are typically used in the calculation.

How to Interpret:
    Readings over +0.55 are considered bullish. Readings under +.045 are viewed as bearish.

Chart Example:
    Figure 17–3 provides a comparison of the Breadth Advance/Decline Indicator versus the Standard & Poor's 500 Index.

Figure 17–2
10-Day Simple Moving Average
of the Advance/Decline Noncumulative (Top)
versus the Standard & Poor's 500 Index (Bottom)

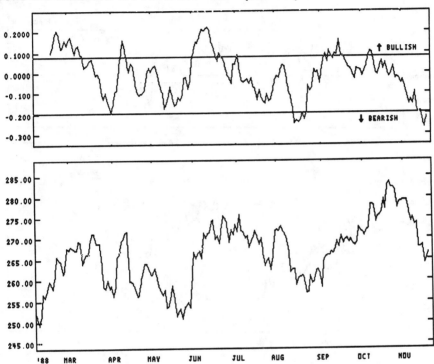

Volume Indicators

Cumulative Volume Index

How to Calculate:
The Cumulative Volume Index is a running total of upside minus down-side volume. First, subtract the volume of declining issues from the volume of advancing issues. Then, add that net volume figure to the cumulative value for the previous period. Daily New York Stock Exchange data are typically used in the calculation.

Figure 17–3
Breadth Advance/Decline Indicator (Top)
versus the Standard & Poor's 500 Index (Bottom)

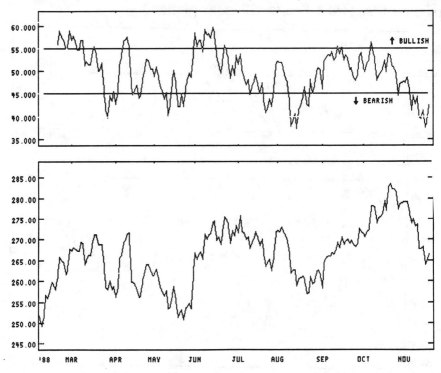

How to Interpret:

As with the Advance-Decline Line, the trend of the Cumulative Volume Index is more important than its actual value. The Cumulative Volume Index is visually compared to a market index (such as the Standard & Poor's 500 Index) for divergences. Underlying market strength (a bullish sign) is suggested if the Cumulative Volume Index is rising at a time when the market index is declining. On the other hand, underlying market weakness (a bearish sign) is in place if the Cumulative Volume Index is declining while the market index rises.

Chart Example:

Figure 17–4 provides a comparison of the Cumulative Volume Index versus the Standard & Poor's 500 Index.

Figure 17–4
Cumulative Volume Index (Top)
versus Standard & Poor's 500 Index (Bottom)

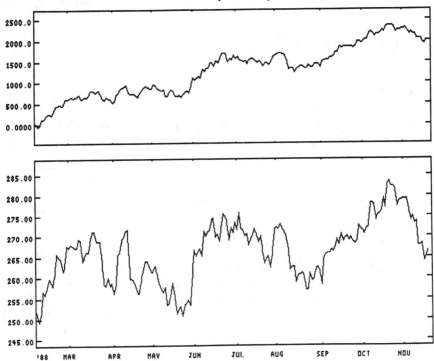

Upside/Downside Ratio

How to Calculate:

The Upside/Downside Ratio is calculated by simply dividing the volume of advancing issues by the volume of declining issues. Daily New York Stock Exchange data are typically used in the calculation.

How to Interpret:

Common interpretation is that high readings are bullish because they indicate buying pressure; low readings are bearish reflecting selling pressure. Since readings of the Upside/Downside Ratio are often erratic from day to day, it is suggested that a moving average be used to smooth the readings and make interpretation more reliable. For example, in calculating a 10-day moving average of the Upside/Downside Ratio, readings over 2.3 are considered to be bullish and readings under 0.75 are viewed as bearish.

Chart Example:

Figure 17–5 provides a comparison of the Upside/Downside Ratio versus the Standard & Poor's 500 Index.

New High/New Low Indicators

High Low Logic Index

The High Low Logic Index was developed by Norman Fosback (The Institute for Econometric Research, 3471 North Federal Highway, Fort Lauderdale, FL 33306).

Figure 17–5
10-Day Simple Moving Average of the Upside/Downside
Ratio (Top) versus the Standard & Poor's 500 Index (Bottom)

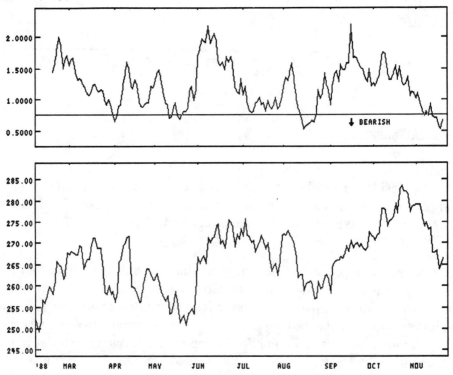

How to Calculate:
The High Low Logic Index is calculated by taking the lesser of the number of new highs or number of new lows and dividing it by the total number of issues traded. Daily or weekly New York Stock Exchange data are typically used in the calculation.

How to Interpret:
High indicator readings occur when many stocks establish new highs at the same time that many stocks reach new lows. This inconsistency in market internals is considered bearish for stock prices.
A uniform market is suggested by extreme low readings of the High Low Logic Index. This is viewed as bullish for stock prices.
Specifically, daily readings under 0.003 are considered to be bullish; daily readings over 0.018 are bearish. Weekly readings under 0.01 are bullish; weekly readings over 0.05 are bearish.

New High/New Low Ratio

How to Calculate:
The New High/New Low Ratio is calculated by simply dividing the number of issues reaching new highs in price by the number of issues reaching new lows in price. New highs and new lows are defined as issues reaching new extremes in price during the last 52 weeks. Daily or weekly New York Stock Exchange data are typically used in the calculation.

How to Interpret:
Extreme high readings (over 20) are considered bullish. Extreme low readings (under 0.06) are bearish.

Chart Example:
Figure 17–6 provides a comparison of the New High/New Low Ratio versus the Standard & Poor's 500 Index.

Sentiment Indicators

Sentiment indicators examine investor expectations and their opinions regarding the stock market. The premise behind sentiment indicators is that the small investor is usually wrong about the direction that the stock market is about to take. Therefore, technicians use these indicators as contrary indica-

Figure 17–6
New High/New Low Ratio (Top)
versus the Standard & Poor's 500 Index (Bottom)

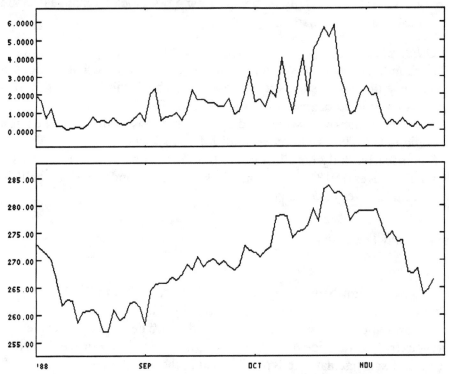

tors. That is, if a sentiment indicator reveals that individual investors believe that the stock market will go up, the market is likely to fall.

Let's examine a few of the popular sentiment indicators in detail.

Advisory Sentiment Index

The Advisory Sentiment Index was developed by A. W. Cohen of Chartcraft, Inc., and it is reported on a weekly basis in a related publication, *Investors Intelligence* (1 West Avenue, Larchmont, NY 10538). *Barron's* also reports the Advisory Sentiment Index readings on a weekly basis.

The Advisory Sentiment Index is a contrary indicator. Based on an analysis of over 100 stock market newsletters, the proportion of bullish and bearish newsletter writers are summarized. At major turning points in the market, advisory services, in aggregate, tend to be wrong about the direction of stock prices. If the vast majority of advisory services are bearish, it is considered a bullish sign for the stock market. On the other hand, if the vast majority of advisory services are bullish, it is viewed as a bearish sign for the stock market.

It is suggested that you smooth weekly readings using a four-week simple moving average to gain a clearer picture of what the indicator is suggesting. When you do so, readings under 37.5 percent are bullish and readings over 75 percent should be considered bearish.

Odd Lot Balance Index

How to Calculate:

The Odd Lot Balance Index is calculated by dividing odd lot sales by odd lot purchases. Daily New York Stock Exchange data are typically used in the calculation.

How to Interpret:

When an investor buys or sells less than 100 shares of stock it is an odd lot. Since this type of activity traditionally was done by small investors who tend to be wrong about the direction of stock prices at market turning points, the Odd Lot Balance Index is designed as a contrary opinion sentiment indicator.

Extreme high daily readings (over 2.5) are considered as bullish. Extreme low daily readings do not signal bullish or bearish times ahead. The reliability of the indicator can be improved by taking a 10-day simple moving average of the daily readings. The resulting readings are considered to be bullish when they exceed 2.35.

Chart Example:

Figure 17–7 provides a comparison of the Odd Lot Balance Index versus the Standard & Poor's 500 Index.

Put/Call Ratio

How to Calculate:

The Put/Call Ratio is calculated by dividing the volume of put options by the volume of call options. Daily Chicago Board Options Exchange (CBOE) data are typically used in the calculation.

Figure 17–7
10-Day Simple Moving Average of the Odd Lot Balance Index (Top)
versus the Standard & Poor's 500 Index (Bottom)

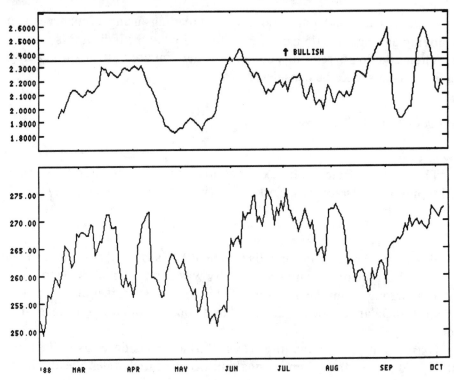

How to Interpret:

Extreme high daily readings (over 0.55) are considered to be bullish. Extreme low daily readings can be viewed as bearish, but are not reliable enough to warrant taking action based on such readings.

Put/Call Ratio signals can be enhanced through the use of a moving average to smooth out daily readings. For example, if you employ a 10-day simple moving average, readings over 0.50 are bullish and those over 0.70 are extremely bullish.

Chart Example:

Figure 17–8 provides a comparison of a 10-day simple moving average of the Put/Call Ratio versus the Standard & Poor's 500 Index.

Figure 17–8
10-Day Simple Moving Average of the Put/Call Ratio (Top)
versus the Standard & Poor's 500 Index (Bottom)

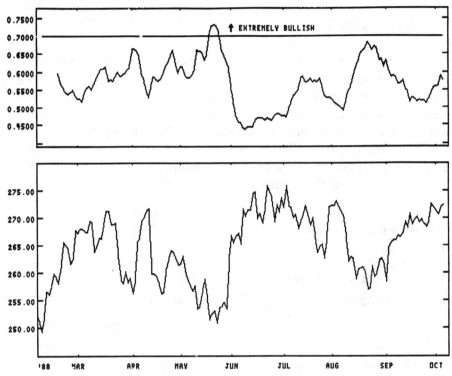

Specialist Short Ratio

How to Calculate:

The Specialist Short Ratio is computed by dividing total specialist short sales by total short sales. Weekly New York Stock Exchange data are typically used in the calculation.

How to Interpret:

Stock exchange "specialists" are responsible for balancing incoming buy and sell orders to maintain orderly markets in the stocks in which they specialize. Specialists, in aggregate, have earned a reputation as particularly astute traders.

Since specialists are normally right and other investors are usually wrong about the direction of stock market prices at major turning points, low Specialist Short Ratio readings are considered to be bullish and high readings are viewed as bearish. In particular, readings under 0.40 are bullish and readings over 0.60 are bearish.

Monetary Indicators

Monetary indicators are based on the concept that an inverse relationship exists between interest rates and the stock market. The logic is that investors want their money in the vehicle most likely to yield the greatest return. If interest rates decline, the yield from investments such as bonds, money market funds, and certificates of deposits also decline. Therefore, stocks become more attractive as the likelihood increases that their return on investment will be greater than that of interest-bearing investments.

A discussion of three reliable monetary indicators follows.

Fed Funds-Discount Rate Spread Index

How to Calculate:

The Fed Funds-Discount Rate Spread Index is simply the difference between the Federal Funds Rate and the Discount Rate. Weekly data are typically used in the calculation.

How to Interpret:

Discount Rate increases and cuts usually trail changes in the Federal Funds Rate. Therefore, the probability of a Discount Rate increase or cut becomes greater as the spread widens.

Since increases in the Discount Rate are generally bearish for stock prices, a positive spread (particularly greater than 3.0) is considered to be bearish. On the other hand, decreases in the Discount Rate are generally bullish for stock prices, and a negative spread (particularly less than -0.3) is viewed as bullish.

Three Steps and a Stumble

The Three Steps and a Stumble rule is a monetary indicator developed by Edson Gould. It states that when the Federal Reserve increases any one of three items (the discount rate, margin requirement, or reserve requirement) three times in a row, stock prices will "stumble" and fall.

Norman Fosback (The Institute for Econometric Research, 3471 North Federal Highway, Fort Lauderdale, FL 33306) noted that between 1914 and

1983, 12 sell signals were given by the Three Steps and a Stumble rule. The results are summarized in the following table:

Time Period	Average Percent Change in S&P 500	Number of Times Market Declined
20 days later	-1.4	5 out of 12
3 months later	-0.3	6 out of 12
6 months later	-1.1	6 out of 12
1 year later	-5.0	8 out of 12

Additionally, Fosback discovered that substantial decreases in stock prices (about 30 percent on average) followed all sell signals.

This indicator is a warning sign that prices are likely to decline significantly. It should not be used for precise timing of market tops.

Two Tumbles and a Jump

The Two Tumbles and a Jump rule was developed in 1973 by Norman Fosback (The Institute for Econometric Research, 3471 North Federal Highway, Fort Lauderdale, FL 33306). It states that when the Federal Reserve decreases any one of three items (the discount rate, margin requirement, or reserve requirement) two times in a row, stock prices will "jump". Fosback's research shows that between 1914 and 1983, 17 buy signals were given by the Two Tumbles and a Jump rule.

The results are summarized in the following table:

Time Period	Average Percent Change in S&P 500	Number of Times Market Advanced
20 days later	+ 3.6	13 out of 17
3 months later	+11.3	14 out of 17
6 months later	+17.1	16 out of 17
1 year later	+30.5	16 out of 17

Combining Indicators into a Model

Most technicians follow more than one technical market indicator. Often, they combine several indicators into a model. The objective is to gain a consensus view of whether stocks will go up or down, rather than relying on a single indicator (since all indicators give their share of false signals). When combining indicators into a model, each component indicator can be weighted equally, or more weight can be given to those indicators deemed to be more reliable.

True or False Quiz

Circle T if the statement is true or F if the statement is false.

T   F   1. Technical market indicators are used to determine the trend of individual stocks.

T   F   2. When the Standard & Poor's 500 Index is rising at the same time that the Advance-Decline Line is falling, the outlook for the stock market is bearish.

T   F   3. The Upside/Downside Ratio is calculated by dividing the number of advancing issues by the number of declining issues.

T   F   4. The small investor is usually wrong about the direction that the stock market is about to take.

T   F   5. Stocks become more attractive to investors as interest rates decline.

T   F   6. Certain technical market indicators are always right about the direction of stock market prices.

Answers

1. *False.* Technical market indicators are used to determine the trend of the overall stock market, not individual stocks.

2. *True.*

3. *False.* The Upside/Downside Ratio is calculated by dividing the volume (not the number) of advancing issues by the volume of declining issues.

4. *True.*

5. *True.*

6. *False.* Even the most reliable indicators give false signals.

PUTTING IT ALL TOGETHER

A Structured Approach to Technical Analysis

The first 17 lessons presented the basic, as well as some advanced, tools that the technician uses for market analysis. In the final two lessons of this course, these concepts will be tied together into a structured approach to technical analysis. Lesson 18 outlines the approach and Lesson 19 demonstrates how to apply it under real market conditions.

A top down approach to market analysis is presented. The overall market is examined first, then the industry (or commodity) group is analyzed, and finally the individual security (stock or commodity) is evaluated. In addition, each component should be looked at first from a long-term perspective and then from intermediate- and short-term perspectives, depending on your investment time horizon.

Stocks

Analyzing stocks in a structured fashion is a three-step process. First, examine the overall stock market keeping in mind that most stocks move in the same direction as the overall stock market. Second, analyze the industry group of which the stock is a part. Finally, the stock itself is analyzed for bullish or bearish implications.

Tables 18–1, 18–2, and 18–3 present structured approaches to analyzing the overall market, industry groups, and individual securities, respectively. Some steps are basic and almost always performed. Other steps are optional and performed as a result of personal preference or to supplement the basic steps when they do not, by themselves, provide a clear picture of the trend of prices.

Options

For options, follow the same steps as for stocks. Upon completion of those steps, decide whether the outlook for the particular stock is bullish or bearish. Once that basic decision is made, selection of a specific option contract can be made using one or more of the popular option strategies.

Commodities

The approach presented for stocks is equally applicable to commodities. Simply substitute the words *overall commodity market, commodity group,* and *individual commodity contract* for *overall stock market, industry group,* and *individual stock,* respectively. Then perform the same steps as you would for stocks.

Final Thoughts

The structured approach is only one of many combinations of technical analysis tools and techniques available. It can be used to begin. As one gains more experience and becomes more comfortable with the various steps, the approach can be customized to fit one's individual investment philosophy.

Table 18-1
Overall Market Analysis:
A Structured Approach to Technical Analysis

Step Number	Basic/ Optional	Description	Lesson Reference
1	Basic	Construct a bar chart of a market index (such as, the Standard & Poor's 500 Index).	2
2	Basic	Examine the bar chart for the following types of chart patterns:	
		Reversal	3
		Consolidation	4
		Gaps	5
3	Basic	Draw trendlines and support and resistance lines, if applicable, on the bar chart.	6,7
4	Optional	Draw trend channels, fan lines, percentage retracement levels, and speed resistance lines, if applicable, on the bar chart.	6,7
5	Basic	Calculate and plot a simple moving average of closing prices on the bar chart.	8
6	Optional	Calculate and plot weighted, exponential, and multiple moving averages on the bar chart.	8
7	Optional	Plot envelopes (trading bands) on the bar chart.	8
8	Optional	Perform an analysis of the level of volume.	10
9	Optional	Calculate and analyze on-balance volume.	10
10	Optional	Analyze volume using the Volume Reversal technique.	10
11	Optional	Calculate and analyze momentum, rate of change, and moving average oscillators.	11
12	Optional	Calculate and analyze the Relative Strength Index.	12
13	Optional	Calculate and analyze Stochastics.	13
14	Optional	Plot price data on a point and figure chart. Examine for various types of chart patterns. Draw trendlines and support and resistance lines.	14
15	Optional	Construct a Japanese candlestick chart. Examine for various types of chart patterns.	15
16	Basic	Analyze various technical market indicators.	17
17	Optional	Determine whether the Dow Theory is bullish or bearish.	16

Table 18–2
Industry Group Analysis:
A Structured Approach to Technical Analysis

Step Number	Basic/ Optional	Description	Lesson Reference
1	Basic	Perform relative strength analysis comparing an industry group to a market index (such as, the Standard & Poor's 500 Index).	9
2	Basic	Construct a bar chart of the industry group.	2
3	Basic	Examine the bar chart for the following types of chart patterns:	
		Reversal	3
		Consolidation	4
		Gaps	5
4	Optional	Draw trendlines and support and resistance lines, if applicable, on the bar chart.	6,7
5	Basic	Draw trend channels, fan lines, percentage retracement levels, and speed resistance lines, if applicable, on the bar chart.	6,7
6	Optional	Calculate and plot a simple moving average of closing prices on the bar chart.	8
7	Optional	Calculate and plot weighted, exponential, and multiple moving averages on the bar chart.	8
8	Optional	Plot envelopes (trading bands) on the bar chart.	8
9	Optional	Calculate and analyze momentum, rate of change, and moving average oscillators.	11
10	Optional	Calculate and analyze the Relative Strength Index.	12
11	Optional	Calculate and analyze Stochastics.	13
12	Optional	Plot price data on a point and figure chart. Examine for various types of chart patterns. Draw trendlines and support and resistance lines.	14
13	Optional	Construct a Japanese candlestick chart. Examine for various types of chart patterns.	15

Table 18–3
Individual Security Analysis:
A Structured Approach to Technical Analysis

Step Number	Basic/ Optional	Description	Lesson Reference
1	Basic	Perform relative strength analysis comparing a security to its industry group or to a market index.	9
2	Basic	Construct a bar chart of the security.	2
3	Basic	Examine the bar chart for the following types of chart patterns:	
		Reversal	3
		Consolidation	4
		Gaps	5
4	Basic	Draw trendlines and support and resistance lines, if applicable, on the bar chart.	6,7
5	Optional	Draw trend channels, fan lines, percentage retracement levels, and speed resistance lines, if applicable, on the bar chart.	6,7
6	Basic	Calculate and plot a simple moving average of closing prices on the bar chart.	8
7	Optional	Calculate and plot weighted, exponential, and multiple moving averages on the bar chart.	8
8	Optional	Plot envelopes (trading bands) on the bar chart.	8
9	Optional	Perform an analysis of the level of volume.	10
10	Optional	Calculate and analyze on-balance volume.	10
11	Optional	Analyze volume using the Volume Reversal technique.	10
12	Optional	Calculate and analyze momentum, rate of change, and moving average oscillators.	11
13	Optional	Calculate and analyze the Relative Strength Index.	12
14	Optional	Calculate and analyze Stochastics.	13
15	Optional	Plot price data on a point and figure chart. Examine for various types of chart patterns. Draw trendlines and support and resistance lines.	14
16	Optional	Construct a Japanese candlestick chart. Examine for various types of chart patterns.	15

LESSON 19

A Final Case Study

As the final lesson of this course, it is only fitting that real market conditions be analyzed using the tools and techniques presented thus far. Therefore, an analysis of the overall stock market, an industry group (the Food — Sugar & Refining Industry Group), and a particular stock in that industry group (Savannah Foods) will be performed in the manner suggested in Lesson 18.

The 36 charts used for analytical purposes were all generated as of December 9, 1988. For the most part, the charts speak for themselves. Examine them closely and read the descriptive information accompanying each to learn what they convey. Following the charts, a summary of findings that ties all of the results together is presented.

Note that although the analysis presented applies to the stock market, the same techniques can be used to analyze other markets. For example, for commodities, instead of analyzing the overall stock market, industry groups, and individual stocks, one would examine the overall commodity market (using the Commodity Research Bureau (CRB) Index), commodity groups (such as, grains), and particular commodities (such as, soybeans).

Overall Market Analysis

The charts presented in Figures 19–1 through 19–20 provide an analysis of the overall stock market.

Figure 19–1
The overall stock market (as illustrated here using the Standard &
Poor's 500 Index) has been in a clearly defined uptrend since 1982.
Therefore, from a long-term perspective, the overall stock market's
trend is up.

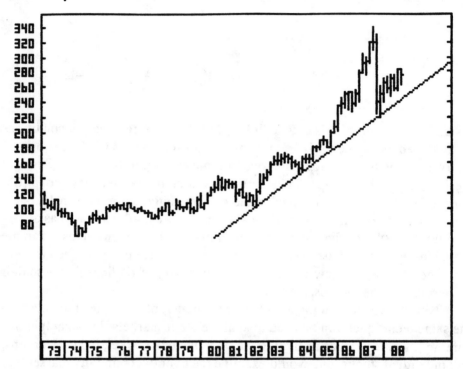

Source: By permission of Telescan, Inc.

Figure 19–2
During the 1987 stock market crash, 50 percent of the gain from August 1982 to August 1987 was retraced. A 50 percent retracement is not an unusual amount for a correction and is not enough to change the long-term trend from up to down.

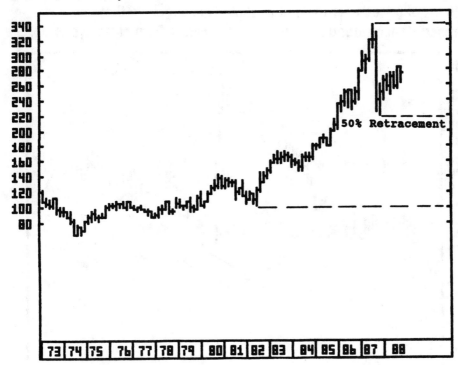

Source: By permission of Telescan, Inc.

Figure 19–3
A three-year bar chart of the overall market (as illustrated here using the Standard & Poor's 500 Index) pictures a sideways trend from an intermediate-term perspective. A less than well defined symmetrical triangle pattern can be spotted with an upside breakout and subsequent pullback of prices near the end of 1988. This suggests that the intermediate-term trend may be about to change from sideways to up.

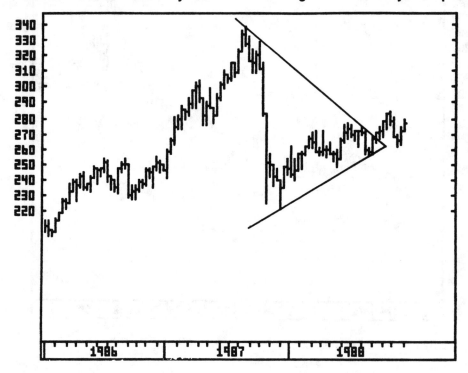

Source: By permission of Telescan, Inc.

Figure 19–4
The overall market is currently above its 40-week simple moving average which is viewed as a bullish sign.

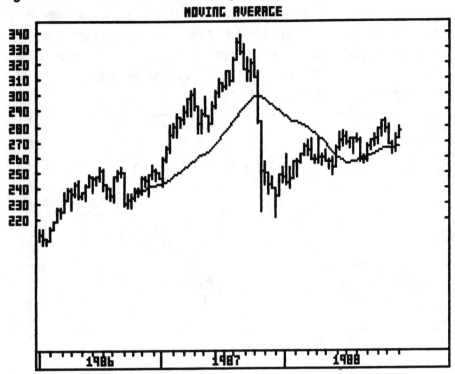

Source: By permission of Telescan, Inc.

Figure 19–5
The overall market has retraced approximately 55 percent of the drop in
prices from the August 1987 peak to the 1987 low. A further retracement
that results in more than ⅔ of the drop in prices being retraced would
be viewed as very bullish. Failure to retrace more than ⅔ of the drop in
prices would suggest bearish implications. A wait and see attitude must
be maintained with respect to whether the intermediate-term will change
from sideways to up or sideways to down.

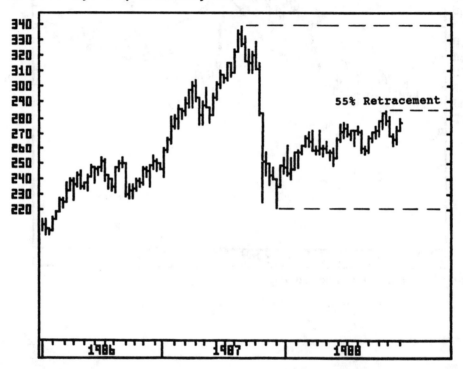

Source: By permission of Telescan, Inc.

Figure 19–6
A one-year bar chart of the overall stock market
(as illustrated here using the Standard & Poor's 500 Index)
shows prices in a well defined up trend channel.

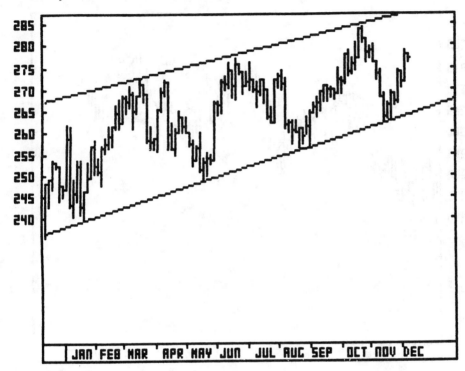

Source: By permission of Telescan, Inc.

Figure 19–7
The overall stock market has fluctuated just above and below its 10-day simple moving average throughout the last year. Currently, prices are above the moving average which is considered bullish.

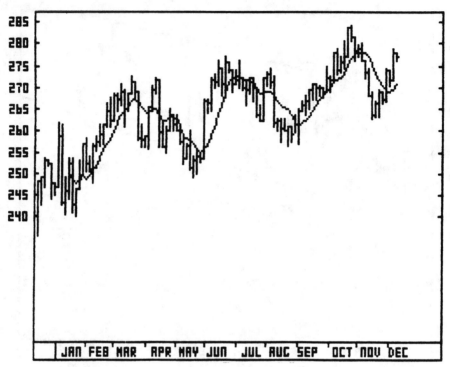

Source: By permission of Telescan, Inc.

Figure 19–8
A 10-day momentum oscillator (plotted at the bottom of the chart) has moved up over the past month, a bullish sign.

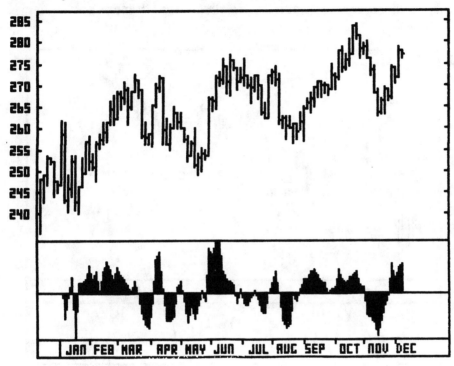

Source: By permission of Telescan, Inc.

Figure 19–9
A 15-day Relative Strength Index (plotted at the bottom of the chart) is
trending sharply higher. Since stock prices are also moving higher,
there is no divergence between the Relative Strength Index and
stock prices.

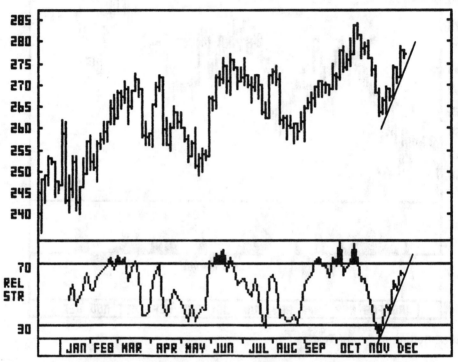

Source: By permission of Telescan, Inc.

Figure 19–10
**A Stochastics plot (%D line shown at the bottom of the chart) is moving
higher along with prices (plotted at the top of the chart).**

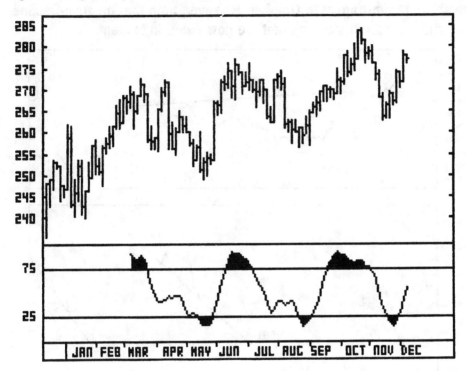

Source: By permission of Telescan, Inc.

Figure 19–11
The Advance-Decline Line (top of chart) was at a bearish divergence to
the Standard & Poor's 500 Index (bottom of chart—closing prices only
are shown) from August to October. However, both the Advance-Decline
Line and the overall stock market are now rising in tandem.

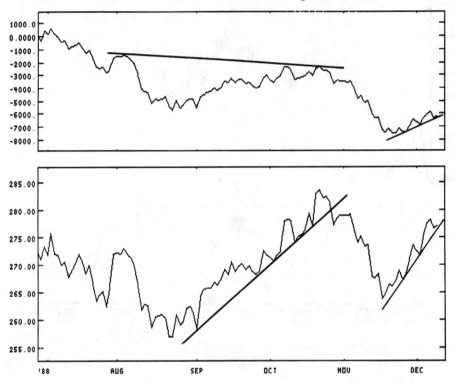

Figure 19–12
The 10-day simple moving average of the Advance/Decline Noncumulative indicator (top of chart) is currently at a bullish level.

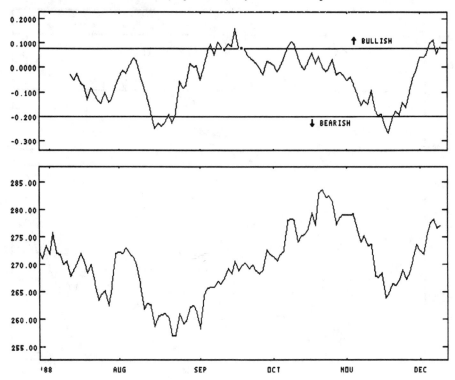

Figure 19–13
The Breadth Advance/Decline Indicator (top of chart)
is currently at a neutral level.

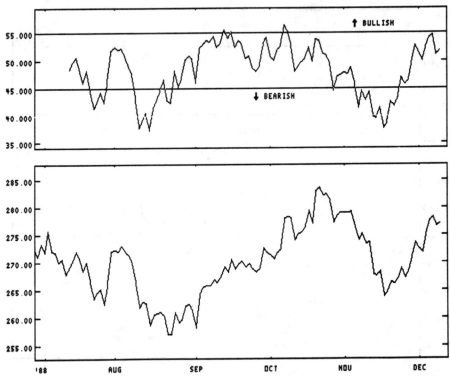

Figure 19–14
The Cumulative Volume Index (top of chart) has moved in the same direction as the Standard & Poor's 500 Index (bottom of chart—closing prices only are shown) throughout the past few months. No divergences are noted.

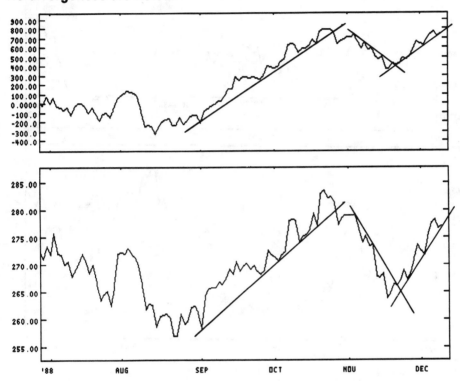

Figure 19–15
A 10-day simple moving average of the Upside/Downside Ratio
(top of chart) has moved from a bearish to a neutral reading
over the last few weeks.

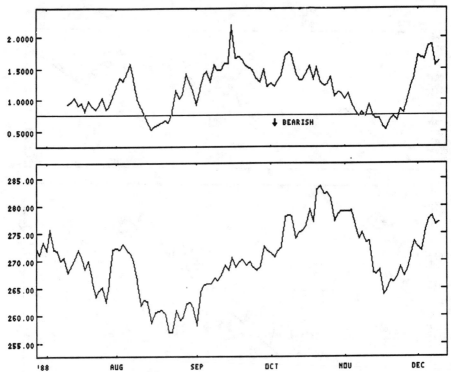

Figure 19–16
The New High/High Low Ratio (top of chart) has moved
from a bearish to a neutral reading over the last few weeks.

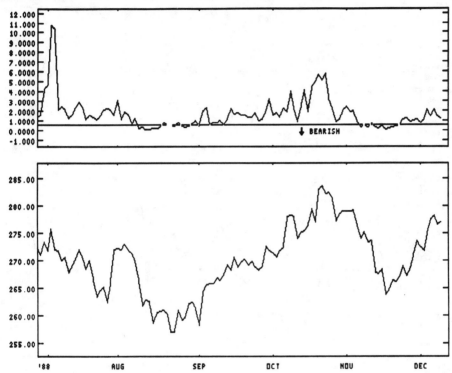

Figure 19–17
A 10-day simple moving average of the Odd Lot Balance Index
(top of chart) has just moved from a bullish to a neutral reading.

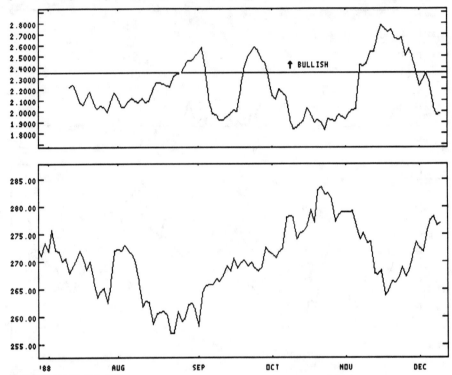

Figure 19–18
A 10-day simple moving average of the Put/Call Ratio
(top of chart) has been at a bullish level for the past few weeks.

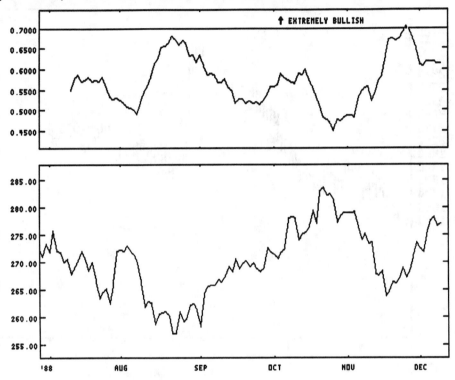

Figure 19–19
The Dow Jones Industrial Average rose above the high of its previous upward secondary reaction during 1988 (at point A on the chart).

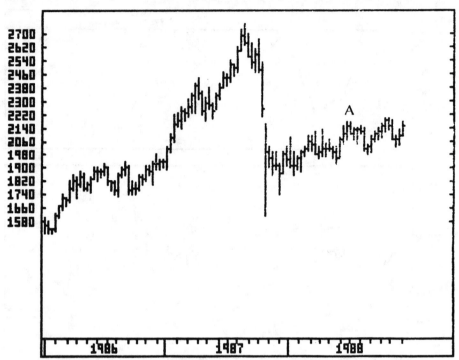

Source: By permission of Telescan, Inc.

Figure 19–20
The Dow Jones Transportation Average confirmed the
Dow Theory bull trend signaled by the Dow Jones Industrial Average by
reaching a new high at point B on the chart.

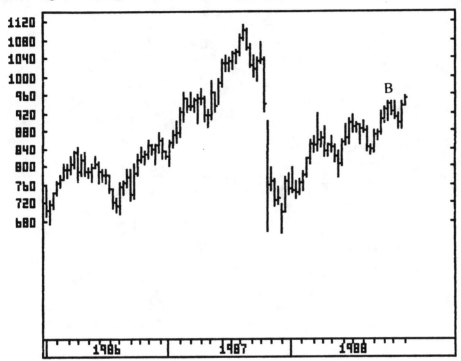

Source: By permission of Telescan, Inc.

Industry Analysis

The charts presented in Figures 19–21 through 19–24 reflect industry group activity.

Figure 19–21
The Food—Sugar & Refining Industry Group Index has
been in a clearly defined uptrend since 1980. Therefore, from a long-
term perspective, the Food—Sugar & Refining Industry's trend is up.

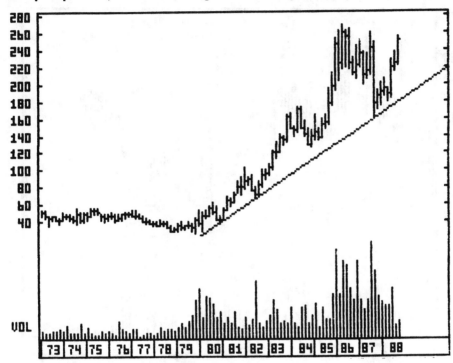

Source: By permission of Telescan, Inc.

Figure 19–22
A three-year bar chart of the Food—Sugar & Refining
Industry Group shows sideways action with prices
trending higher over the past few months.

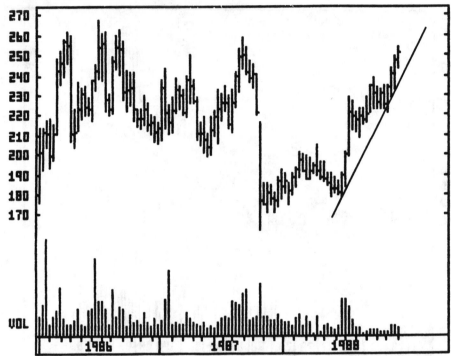

Source: By permission of Telescan, Inc.

Figure 19–23
A one-year chart of the Food—Sugar & Refining Industry Group Index
shows an up-trend in prices since June.
Note the flag chart pattern after the quick ascent in prices
in June and July. At the end of the period shown,
prices are moving sharply higher.

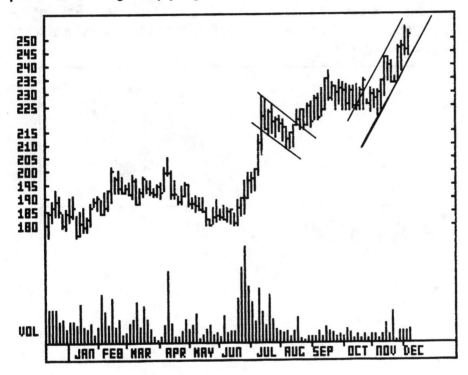

Source: By permission of Telescan, Inc.

Figure 19–24
The relative strength of the Food—Sugar & Refining Industry Group Index versus the overall stock market (as represented by the Standard & Poor's 500 Index) is shown below. Below the horizontal line reflects underperformance of the industry group versus the overall market; above the horizontal line shows overperformance of the industry group versus the overall market. The Food—Sugar & Refining Industry Group Index has dramatically outperformed the overall market for the past few months.

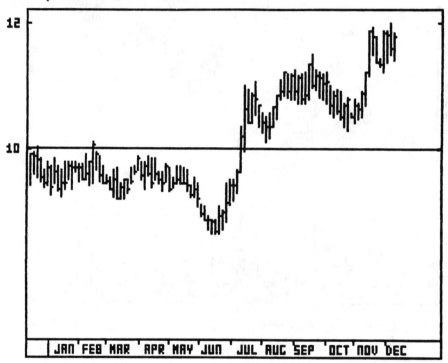

Source: By permission of Telescan, Inc.

Individual Stock Analysis

Figures 19–25 through 19–36 view a particular stock (Savannah Foods) from a variety of perspectives.

Figure 19–25
**Savannah Foods has been in a clearly defined uptrend
since 1980. Therefore, from a long-term perspective,
Savannah Foods' trend is up.**

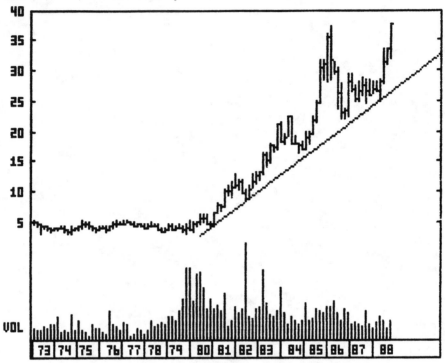

Source: By permission of Telescan, Inc.

Figure 19–26
A three-year bar chart shows that Savannah Foods was in a rectangle chart pattern (otherwise known as a trading range) for most of 1987 and the first half of 1988. A breakout completed a bullish rectangle chart pattern in mid-1988. Note that after the breakout, a normal pullback to the top of the rectangle chart pattern occurred.

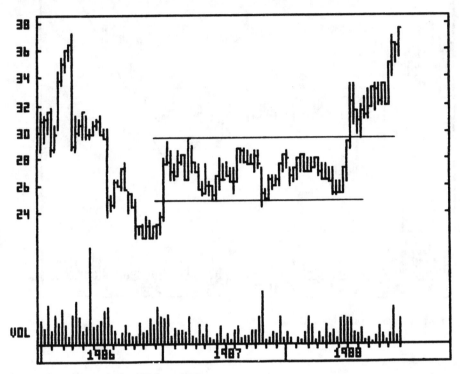

Source: By permission of Telescan, Inc.

Figure 19–27
**Over the second half of 1988, Savannah Foods has been
in an uptrend.**

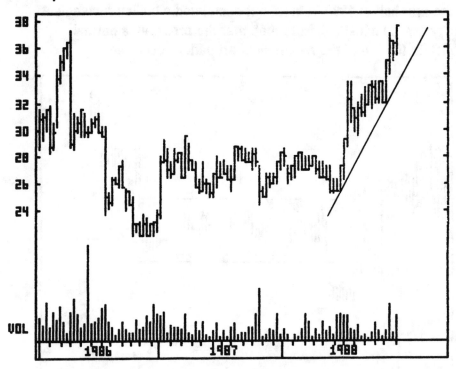

Source: By permission of Telescan, Inc.

Figure 19–28
During the up movement in the second half of 1988,
resistance was met and broken at approximately
the $34 per share level.

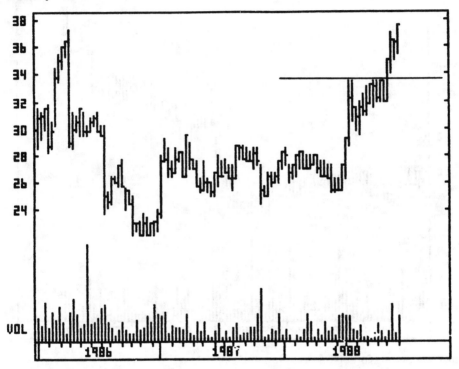

Source: By permission of Telescan, Inc.

Figure 19–29
A one-year bar chart of Savannah Foods provides a
short-term picture of price and volume activity.

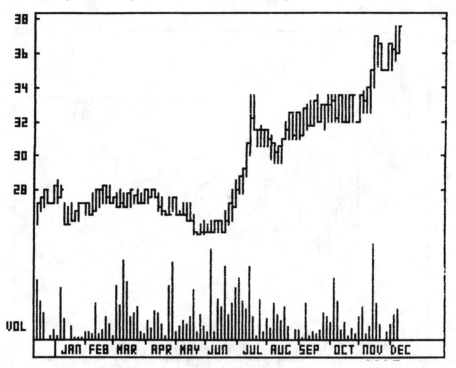

Source: By permission of Telescan, Inc.

Figure 19–30
The relative strength of Savannah Foods versus its industry group
(Food—Sugar & Refining Industry Group Index)
is shown below. Below the horizontal line reflects
underperformance of the stock versus the industry group; above the
horizontal line shows overperformance
versus the industry group. Savannah Foods has
under-performed its industry group for most of the last year.

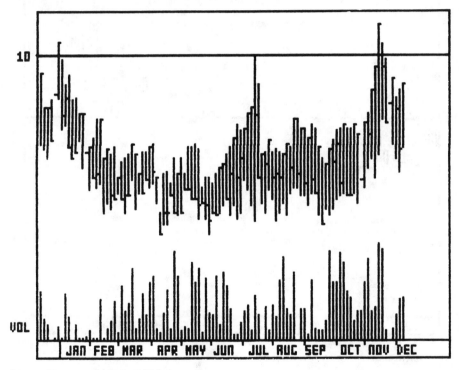

Source: By permission of Telescan, Inc.

Figure 19–31
Although Savannah Foods underperformed its industry group for most of
the last year, it outperformed the overall market significantly throughout
the second half of 1988. Below the horizontal line reflects underperformance of the stock versus the overall market (as represented by
the Standard & Poor's 500 Index); above the horizontal line shows
overperformance of the stock versus the overall market.

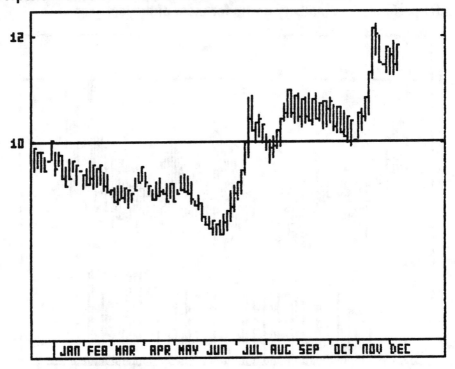

Source: By permission of Telescan, Inc.

Figure 19–32
Support and resistance levels are drawn on the one-year
bar chart of Savannah Foods. Also, note the flag chart
pattern that appeared in July and August.

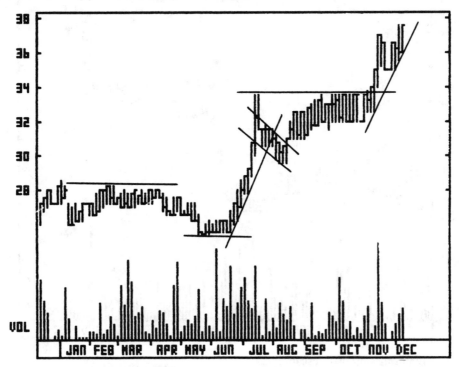

Source: By permission of Telescan, Inc.

Figure 19–33
Savannah Foods' stock price is currently above its 20-day simple moving average, a bullish sign.

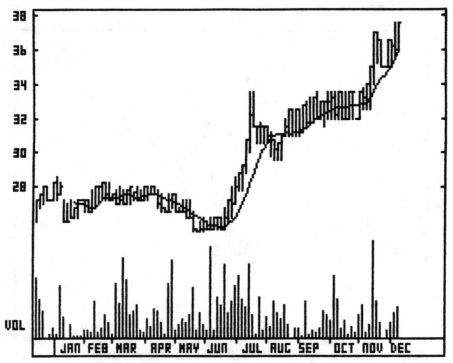

Source: By permission of Telescan, Inc.

Figure 19–34
A 10-day momentum indicator (plotted at the bottom of the chart) is positive for Savannah Foods.

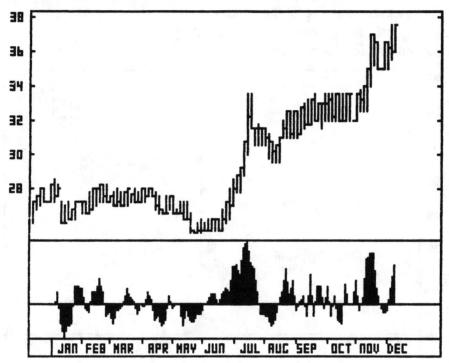

Source: By permission of Telescan, Inc.

Figure 19–35
A 15-day Relative Strength Index (plotted at the bottom
of the chart) is trending upward along with Savannah Foods' stock
price. However, crossing of the 70 line
does suggest that the stock may be reaching
an overbought level and caution is warranted.

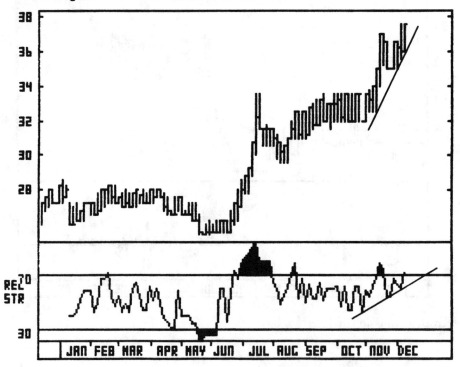

Source: By permission of Telescan, Inc.

Figure 19–36
A stochastics plot (%D line shown at the bottom of the chart) is moving higher along with prices (plotted at the top of the chart). No divergence is noted.

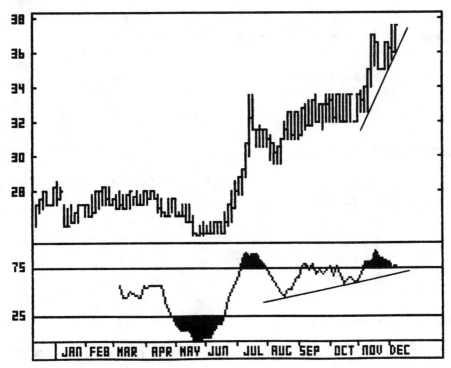

Source: By permission of Telescan, Inc.

Summary of Findings

Overall Market Analysis

The analysis shows that the current trends for the various time horizons (as of the time of the analysis) are as follows:

Time Horizon	Trend Direction
Long-term	Up
Intermediate-term	Sideways
Short-term	Up

Industry Analysis

Results of the analysis of the Food—Sugar & Refining Industry Group Index suggest the following:

Time Horizon	Trend Direction
Long-term	Up
Intermediate-term	Up
Short-term	Up

Individual Stock Analysis

Technical analysis of Savannah Foods results in the following trend conclusions:

Time Horizon	Trend Direction
Long-term	Up
Intermediate-term	Up
Short-term	Up

Should you buy Savannah Foods stock? Let's examine the weight of the evidence. On the positive side the following buy factors exist:

1. The long- and short-term trends of the overall stock market are up.

2. The Dow Theory is bullish.

3. The long-, intermediate-, and short-term trends of Food—Sugar & Refining Industry Group Index are up.

4. The long-, intermediate-, and short-term trends of Savannah Foods are up.

5. On a relative strength basis, Savannah Foods is outperforming the overall market.

On the negative side are the following factors:

1. Although the long- and short-term trends of the overall stock market are up, the intermediate-term trend is sideways. A further retracement of the drop in prices that occurred in 1987 would strengthen a bullish outlook. Currently, 55 percent has been retraced. If in total more than two thirds of the drop was retraced, the intermediate-term trend would change from sideways to up and this negative would turn into a positive.

2. The majority of the technical market indicators are neutral (neither bullish nor bearish).

3. The Relative Strength Index is warning of a possible short-term top.

The weight of evidence leads one to be cautiously bullish. Probabilities suggest that the trend in price for Savannah Foods will continue upward. However, a short-term top and corrective reaction could occur at any time.

Those who are short-term oriented could buy the stock but maintain close stop-loss orders to protect themselves in the event of a corrective reaction.

Intermediate-term investors should wait until the intermediate-term trend of the overall market changes from sideways to up and analyze market conditions for Savannah Foods again at that time.

Long-term investors can buy and hold until the long-term uptrend is broken.

Addition to Second Edition

The preceeding analysis was written in early-December 1988 and included, as is, in the first edition of this book. It has been left unchanged because it provides strong evidence of the value of technical analysis, in general, and using a structured approach, in particular.

In early-December 1988, the weight of evidence suggested being cautiosly bullish. In hindsight, that analysis proved to be right on target. As shown in Figure 19–37, prices moved sideways in a narrow trading range for a couple of months and then rose sharply higher over the next year with two 2-for-1 stock splits occuring along the way.

Short-term investors that bought the stock in early-December 1988 were able to take advantage of the rapid increase in price during 1989 while, at the same time, being protected against a corrective reaction throughout the consolidation period (December 1988 to February 1989) by the suggested stop-loss order.

Intermediate-term investors would have received evidence of a change in the direction of the intermediate-term trend of the overall market and Savannah Foods from sideways to up very early in 1989 and could have participated in most of the sharp increase in the price of Savannah Foods.

Long-term investors that bought and held the stock also would have found this to be a very profitable investment.

The best test of any investment approach is the test of time and technical analysis. As demonstrated in this real market example, it has clearly proved itself to be a valid and profitable approach to investing.

Figure 19–37
After breaking out of a narrow trading range in February 1989,
the price of Savannah Foods rose sharply until early-1990.

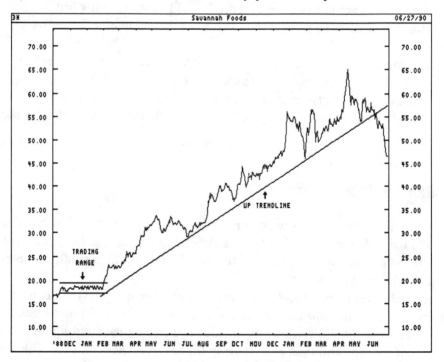

CONGRATULATIONS!

You have reached the end of this course, but hopefully not the end of your study of technical analysis. You can expand upon your knowledge by studying some of the recommended publications listed in the Appendix.

APPENDIX

Sources of Technical Related Information

Financial Newspapers

On a daily basis, the vast majority of information that you need to apply technical analysis principles can be found in both *Investor's Business Daily* and *The Wall Street Journal.*

> *Investor's Business Daily*, 12655 Beatrice Street, Los Angeles, CA 90066.

> *The Wall Street Journal*, Dow Jones & Co., Inc., 200 Burnett Road, Chicopee, MA 01021.

Magazines

> *Barron's*, Dow Jones & Co., Inc., 200 Burnett Road, Chicopee, MA 01021. Extensive technical related information is published on a weekly basis.

> *Futures: The Magazine of Commodities & Options*, 219 Parkade, Cedar Falls, IA 50613. This monthly informational and educational magazine covers futures and options worldwide.

> *Technical Analysis of Stocks & Commodities*, 3517 S.W. Alaska Street, Seattle, WA 98126. This monthly magazine presents regular articles on charting techniques, case studies of trading methods, computer programs for trading, numeric systems, and risk management.

Chart Services

The companies listed below provide charts on a subscription basis (weekly, bi-weekly, monthly, etc.) in a variety of formats. Most chart services offer a trial subscription for a nominal fee to enable you to determine if a particular chart service will be beneficial to you.

Chartcraft, Inc., 30 Church Street, New Rochelle, NY 10801. Types of charts: Specializes in point and figure charts for stocks, commodities and financial futures, options, and technical market indicators.

Commodity Perspective, 30 S. Wacker Drive, Suite 1820, Chicago, IL 60606. Types of charts: Commodities and financial futures.

Commodity Price Charts, A Division of Oster Communications Inc., 219 Parkade, Cedar Falls, IA 50613. Types of charts: Commodities and financial futures.

Commodity Research Bureau, 30 S. Wacker Drive, Suite 1820, Chicago, IL 60606. Types of charts: Commodities and financial futures.

Commodity Trend Service, P.O. Box 32309, Palm Beach Gardens, FL 33420. Types of charts: Commodities and financial futures.

Daily Graphs, William O'Neil & Co., Inc., P.O. Box 24933, Los Angeles, CA 90024. Types of charts: Stocks and options.

Knight-Ridder Commodity Research Bureau, 100 Church Street, Suite 1850, New York, NY 10007. Types of charts: Commodities and financial futures.

R.W. Mansfield Co., Inc., 2973 Kennedy Boulevard, Jersey City, NJ 07306. Type of charts: Stocks.

Securities Research Co., 208 Newbury Street, Boston, MA 02116. Type of charts: Stocks.

Standard & Poor's Corp., 25 Broadway, New York, NY 10024. Type of charts: Stocks.

Recommended Books

There is no question that books provide an excellent way to learn about new techniques and expand your knowledge of technical analysis at a relatively low cost. However, you must be careful when selecting books. Quite frankly, many technical analysis books provide little or no value. These books typically fall into the categories of (1) "get rich quick" trading systems that do not work in real-time trading, (2) those describing techniques in theoretical terms which cannot be practically implemented, and (3) books which are simply poorly written making it difficult to understand the material presented.

The good news is that the remaining books offer a wealth of valuable information. Some of these books were first published decades ago and have stood the test of time, while others have only recently been published.

For your benefit, the author has identified technical analysis books which are, in his opinion, the best. These books are organized alphabetically by title. After each title appears the book's author, number of pages in the book, copyright date, publisher's name, and a brief description of the book's contents.

The Arms Index (TRIN): An Introduction to the Volume Analysis of Stock and Bond Markets, Richard W. Arms, Jr., 100 pages, 1989, Business One Irwin, Homewood, IL. Written by the originator of the Arms Index (commonly known as TRIN). Shows how to calculate and interpret the Arms Index in the stock and other markets. Presents numerous variations on the original Arms Index.

A Complete Guide to the Futures Markets: Fundamental Analysis, Technical Analysis, Trading, Spreads, and Options, Jack D. Schwager, 741 pages, 1984, John Wiley & Sons, Inc., New York, NY. Primarily focuses on fundamental analysis. However, it also includes a good section on chart analysis and systems trading as applied to the futures markets.

Dow Theory Redux: The Classic Investment Theory Revised & Updated for the 1990s, Michael D. Sheimo, 176 pages, 1989, Probus Publishing Co., Chicago, IL. Explains how the Dow Theory, originally developed in the early 1900s, can be used to invest in today's markets.

Elliott Wave Principle: Key to Stock Market Profits (Expanded Edition), Robert R. Prechter, Jr. and A. J. Frost, 249 pages, 1990, New Classics Library, Inc., Gainesville, GA. As the basic handbook of the Elliott Wave Principle, it is must reading for those interested in Elliott techniques. Thoroughly covers all the relevant concepts of the Elliott Wave Principle.

The Encyclopedia of Stock Market Techniques, Investors Intelligence, 744 pages, 1985, Investors Intelligence, New Rochelle, NY. Presents a wide variety of technical analysis concepts and approaches to the stock market. Each chapter is written by an expert on the topic discussed.

The Encyclopedia of Technical Market Indicators, Robert W. Colby and Thomas A. Meyers, 581 pages, 1988, Business One Irwin, Homewood, IL. Presents the most comprehensive description of technical market indicators ever published. Representing thousands of hours of computerized research, it shows the true forecasting value of over 110 indicators.

How Charts Can Help You in the Stock Market, William L. Jiler, 202 pages, 1962, (Reprinted in 1990), Fraser Publishing, Burlington, VT. Provides an excellent introduction to chart pattern analysis. Originally published in 1962 by Trendline (a division of Standard & Poor's Corporation).

How Charts Can Make You Money: Technical Analysis for Investors, T. H. Stewart, 200 pages, 1989, Probus Publishing Co., Chicago, IL. Identifies chart patterns to watch for and how to interpret them. Discusses numerous technical indicators. Presents investment strategies for the long-term investor and for the speculator.

Japanese Candlestick Charting Techniques: A Contemporary Guide to the Ancient Investment Techniques of the Far East, Steve Nison, 310 pages, 1991, New York Institute of Finance, New York, NY. Best for learning about Japanese candlestick charting. Teaches drawing and interpreting over 50 candlestick lines and formations. Shows how to use candlestick charting in conjunction with various other technical analysis techniques. Hundreds of real market examples are included.

The Japanese Chart of Charts, Seiki Shimizu, 206 pages, 1986, published by Tokyo Futures Trading Publishing Company, distributed by Windsor Books, Brightwaters, NY. An English translation of a Japanese book. Discusses origins of various Japanese charting methods. Presents the basics of candlestick chart construction. Describes numerous candlestick chart patterns to watch for and the proper way to interpret them. Finally, a variety of other chart related topics are discussed.

The Major Works of R. N. Elliott, Robert R. Prechter, Jr., Editor, 243 pages, 1980, New Classics Library, Inc., Gainesville, GA. Three ground-breaking works of Ralph Nelson Elliott are combined in this volume (The Wave Principle — 1938; The Financial World — 1939; and, Nature's Law — The Secret of the Universe — 1946).

Market Wizards: Interviews with Top Traders, Jack D. Swager, 458 pages, 1989, New York Institute of Finance, New York, NY. Presents interviews with top professional traders in a variety of markets. Explains the elements of their successes, the different approaches used in different markets, and the trading rules that each trader uses.

New Concepts in Technical Trading Systems, J. Welles Wilder, Jr., 141 pages, 1978, Trend Research, McLeansville, NC. This classic 1978 work presents several unique technical trading systems. It is the original source for the Relative Strength Index, which is very popular among knowledgeable technicians.

New Methods for Profit in the Stock Market, Garfield A. Drew, 384 pages, 1955, Fraser Publishing Company, Burlington, VT. Analyzes specific methods for stock market timing. Although originally published in 1955, the vast majority of concepts remains applicable to the stock market today.

Profits in the Stock Market, Harold M. Gartley, 446 pages, 1981, Traders Press Inc., Greenville, SC. A reprint of H. M. Gartley's 1935 classic on technical analysis. An outstanding supplemental package of charts is included. Particularly useful to those interested in studying stock market activity during the years before and after the great crash of 1929.

Stock Market Logic: A Sophisticated Approach to Profits on Wall Street, Norman G. Fosback, 384 pages, 1990, The Institute for Econometric Research, Fort Lauderdale, FL. Considered to be a current-day classic. It presents well researched conclusions relating to numerous stock market indicators.

Technical Analysis Explained: The Successful Investor's Guide to Spotting Investment Trends and Turning Points (3rd Edition), Martin J. Pring, 521 pages, 1991, McGraw-Hill Publishing Co., New York, NY. Presents a good overview of technical analysis basics and their application to various markets. Focuses on the relationships between interest rates and the stock market.

Technical Analysis of the Futures Markets: A Comprehensive Guide to Trading Methods and Applications, John J. Murphy, 556 pages, 1986, New York Institute of Finance, New York, NY. Provides comprehensive coverage of technical analysis techniques. Includes over 400 chart examples. Don't let the title fool you; the vast majority of techniques discussed is as applicable to the stock market as it is to the futures markets.

Technical Analysis of Stock Trends (6th Edition), Robert D. Edwards and John Magee, 494 pages, 1991, International Technical Analysis, Inc., Boston, MA. Many knowledgeable technicians consider this to be the best book on chart patterns ever written. Necessary reading for any serious student of technical analysis.

Technical Analysis of Stocks, Options & Futures: Advanced Trading Systems and Techniques, William F. Eng, 465 pages, 1988, Probus Publishing Co., Chicago, IL. Examines 15 technical trading techniques. Explains the philosophy behind each technique. Shows how and when to use each of the 15 methods.

Three-Point Reversal Method of Point & Figure Construction and Formations, Michael L. Burke, 107 pages, 1990, Chartcraft, Inc., New Rochelle, NY. Essential reading for current-day point and figure chartists.

Trading Rules: Strategies for Success, William F. Eng, 266 pages, 1990, Dearborn Trade, Chicago, IL. A collection of 50 practical strategies for investing. Filled with proven principles that can lead to long-term trading profits.

Using Stochastics, Cycles & R.S.I., George C. Lane, 50 pages, 1986, Investment Educators, IL. Provides specific guidance on how to use stochastics, cycles, and RSI in a variety of markets. Written by the originator of stochastics.

Volume Cycles in the Stock Market: Market Timing through Equivolume Charting, Richard W. Arms, Jr., 141 pages, 1983, Business One Irwin, Homewood, IL. Describes how Arms uses trading volume to forecast price changes. Stresses that price change cycles are not influenced by the times, but by the trading volume of the stock market. Two original concepts, Volume Cyclicality and Ease of Movement, are explained in detail and their relationships to Equivolume charting are shown.

Winning Market Systems, Gerald Appel, 231 pages, 1989, Windsor Books, Brightwaters, NY. An excellent collection of stock market related trading ideas.

Recommended Technical Analysis Software

All of the charts used as illustrations in this course were prepared using three personal computer technical analysis software packages, namely *MetaStock Professional*, *The Technician*, and *Telescan Analyzer*. In addition, *Compu Trac* is listed below as a recommended technical analysis software package. Before purchasing one of these packages for your personal use, it is suggested that you obtain a demonstration package from the vendor to ensure that it will meet your individual needs.

Compu Trac, Compu Trac, Inc. 1017 Pleasant St., New Orleans, LA 70115. A comprehensive, powerful, and flexible technical analysis program for the most serious technician.

MetaStock Professional, EQUIS International, 3950 South 700 East, Suite 100, Salt Lake City, UT 84107. An excellent and relatively inexpensive charting package with extensive technical analysis capabilities.

The Technician, EQUIS International, 3950 South 700 East, Suite 100, Salt Lake City, UT 84107. Allows you to track over 70 popular technical market indicators.

Telescan Analyzer, Telescan, Inc., 10550 Richmond Ave., Suite 250, Houston, TX 77042. Allows you to access Telescan's online database which includes charts depicting from one month to 15 years of historical price data and technical information on thousands of stocks, mutual funds, industry groups, and market indexes.

Many technical analysis software packages are available in addition to those listed above. For descriptions of currently available technical analysis software packages, it is suggested that you obtain a copy of *The Individual Investor's Microcomputer Resource Guide*. This comprehensive guide is updated and published annually by the American Association of Individual Investors (625 N. Michigan Avenue, Chicago, IL 60611).

Glossary

Accumulation   Occurs when the supply of a security is less than the demand.

Bar chart   A chart of price versus time. The vertical axis indicates price; time intervals are marked on the horizontal axis. For each time period, a vertical line denotes the high and low price of the security; a short horizontal protrusion to the right of the vertical line shows the closing price.

Bearish   The belief that market prices will decline.

Bear market   A market when prices are declining.

Bottom   A low for a security or the overall market.

Breadth   The number of stocks advancing minus those declining. When the number of advancing issues exceeds the number of declining issues, the breadth of the market is viewed as bullish. On the other hand, when the number of advancing issues is less than the number of declining issues, breadth is considered to be a bearish sign.

Breakout   A substantial rise in price above a resistance level or decline in price below a support level. When a breakout occurs, a price trend is likely to continue.

Bullish   The belief that market prices will rise.

Bull market   A market when prices are rising.

Buying climax   A sharp price run-up accompanied by extremely high volume created by investors rushing in to buy securities. This often happens at the end of an up price movement and typically represents a good time to sell.

Channel   A trading range between two parallel lines in which prices move. The slope of the channel represents the direction of the trend.

Confirmation   Refers to the comparison of two or more technical indicators to ensure that they are pointing in the same direction and confirming one another.

Congestion area   A sideways trading range where supply and demand balance out.

Consolidation area   A trading range in which prices move until continuing in the same direction as the trend prior to the consolidation area.

Contrary Opinion   A belief opposite of the general public and Wall Street professionals. At major market turning points, the overall consensus of opinion regarding the future direction of security prices is usually wrong. Thus, an investor taking a contrary view can profit at those items.

Correction   When prices move in the opposite direction of a major trend.

Cycle   A price pattern of movement that regularly occurs in a given time interval.

Distribution   Occurs when the demand for a security is less than the supply.

Divergence   Divergence is the opposite of confirmation. It occurs when one indicator points in one direction (such as, up) and another indicator points in another direction (such as, down).

Downtrend   When the price of a security or the overall market is declining.

Envelope   Contains normal price fluctuations. It is shown graphically as parallel lines at certain percentage points above and below a graph of an indicator or study. If the price goes outside the band, the strength or weakness of the trend is extraordinary. Also known as a trading band.

Exhaustion   When buying power is no longer enough to move prices up or when selling power is no longer enough to move prices lower.

False breakout   A breakout of a chart pattern that aborts. To ensure that a breakout is genuine, look for confirmation by the same or other indicators.

Fundamental analysis   An analytical technique for the buying and selling of stocks based on the belief that stock prices are determined by the underlying value of a company in terms of its cash, current assets, and earnings.

Gap   Represents a price range on a chart at which no trading takes place. When a gap occurs in an uptrend, the current period's low is higher than the previous period's high. In a downtrend, a gap appears when the current period's high is lower than the previous period's low.

Momentum   The rate of expansion of a security's price or volume.

Moving average   A tool used to smooth price fluctuations, allowing you to better determine price trends.

Moving average, exponential   Calculated by multiplying the difference between the current period's price and the exponential moving average for the previous period by an exponent, which varies depending on the length of the moving average. You then add the product of that calculation to the previous exponential moving average to arrive at the current period's exponential moving average.

Moving average, simple   Calculated by adding data for a set period of time and dividing the total by the number of periods.

Moving average, weighted   Calculated by averaging data over a set period of time, giving more emphasis to the most recent data.

Odd lot   Stock purchased in units of less than 100 shares.

Odd lot short sales   The amount of stock sold short in odd lots.

On-balance volume (OBV)   A technical indicator that manipulates volume figures. If the stock price falls to a new low and the OBV does not, the indicator is interpreted as being a positive sign; if the stock price rises to a new high and the OBV does not, the indicator is interpreted as being negative.

Optimization   A test performed on historical data to determine what would have resulted in the maximum profit during a given period of time.

Option   The right to buy or sell specific securities at a specified price within a specified time. A call option gives the holder the right to buy; a put option gives the holder the right to sell.

Overbought   The point (after a period of vigorous buying) at which upward momentum in prices can no longer be maintained and prices can be expected to stabilize or decline.

Oversold   The opposite of overbought. It is a point at which downward momentum in prices can no longer be maintained and prices can be expected to remain stable or rise.

Point and figure chart   Records price activity without reference to time and volume. These charts are used to determine the trend in a security's price.

Price objective   The technical appraisal of a security's future value.

Primary trend   The predominant movement of a market (stock, bond, commodity, or other). When it is up, it is known as a bull market. When it is down, it is called a bear market.

Pullback   When a security or the overall market falls back from a previous advance.

Rally   A brisk advance following a decline in prices.

Reaction   A temporary decline following an advance in prices.

Relative strength   A comparison of the performance of two items, such as an individual stock or group of stocks to the overall market. Relative strength analysis helps select stocks that are likely to outperform the overall market.

Resistance level   The price at which sellers tend to sell in sufficient volume to lower the price of a security. For example, if on a few occasions the price of a given stock has risen to around $50 per share and, on each occasion, the price has subsequently dropped, a technical analyst would consider $50 per share to be a resistance level for that stock.

Secondary trend   Market movement in the opposite direction of the primary trend. These are temporary interruptions in a bull or bear market

Selling climax   A sharp price decline accompanied by extremely high volume created by panic stricken investors dumping securities. This often happens at the end of a bear market and typically represents a good time to buy.

Short covering   The process of buying stock to close out a short sale.

Short selling   Selling stock not owned in anticipation of buying it back later at a lower price for a profit.

Specialist   A member of an exchange who maintains an orderly market in one or more securities. The specialist buys or sells for his or her own account when there is a temporary disparity between supply and demand.

Support level   The price at which buyers tend to buy in sufficient volume to raise the price of a given security. For example, if on a few occasions the price of a given stock has dropped to around $25 per share and, on each occasion, the price has subsequently risen, a technical analyst would consider $25 per share to be a support level for that stock.

Technical analysis   The study of stocks and the overall market based on supply and demand. Technical analysts use charts of historical price and volume activity to predict future price movements.

Technician   One who employs technical analysis as a basis for investment decisions.

Top   A high for a security or the overall market.

Trader   One who buys or sells for his or her own account, typically for short-term profits.

Trend   The trend is the direction of a price movement.

Trendline   A straight line on a chart that connects consecutive tops or consecutive bottoms of prices. Trendlines are used to identify levels of support and resistance.

Uptrend   When the price of a security or the overall market is rising.

Volume   The number of shares traded in a security or a market during a period (such as, a day or week).

Volume histogram   Usually accompanies a high-low-close bar chart. Volume is shown at the bottom of the chart by a vertical bar under each period's price data.

Whipsaw   Occurs when the technique that a trader is using produces many buy and sell signals in a small price range that do not follow through in the predicted direction. Whipsaw trades cause the trader to lose money.

Index